2041

THE VOYAGE SOUTH

2001

"Antarctica left a restless longing in my heart beckoning towards an incomprehensible perfection for ever beyond the reach of mortal man. Its overwhelming beauty touches one so deeply that it is like a wound."

Edwin Mickleburgh,
"Beyond the Frozen Sea."

THE SPONSORS

Royal & SunAlliance
Merrill Lynch International
One Thousand Steps
Rabobank
Wijsmuller Groep
Vopak (Koninklijke Van Ommeren)
P&O Nedlloyd
Heerema Group
Philips International
Unilever
International Award for Young People
Miles of Smiles

King George Island on the Antarctic Peninsula.

First published 2000

by 2nd Nature Ltd.
www.2ndNature.co.uk
Mission Antarctica websites:
www.missionantarctica.com
www.TakeTheNextStep.com

Design, Typesetting & Production by :
Hayloft Publishing, Great Skerrygill, South Stainmore,
Kirkby Stephen, Cumbria, CA17 4EU.

Tel. 017683 42300 or Fax. 017683 41568
e-mail: icetalk@icetalk.co.uk
website: www.hayloft.org.uk

ISBN 0 952 328 275

A catalogue record for this book is available
from the British Library

Printed & bound by Lintons Printers, Co. Durham.

Cover photograph - Peter Koronka

CONTENTS

Page No.

1	Introduction	7
2	The Dream	13
3	The Netherlands	16
4	The Sponsors	20
5	The Crown Prince	22
6	UK Crisis	27
7	Captain & Crew	32
8	Crisis Management	36
9	Heading South	41
10	Atlantic Crossing	46
11	South American Coast	54
12	Tierra del Fuego	59
13	Antarctica	64
14	The Russians	72
15	The Voyage Continues	79
16	2041 Technical Details	83
17	Voyage Maps	84
18	Appendices	88

Captain Scott's party at the South Pole, 17 January 1912. The strain of hauling the sledges and the demoralisation of being beaten by Amundsen is clear on their faces. Left to right, Oates, Bowers (seated), Scott, Wilson (seated), Edgar Evans.

An Introduction

This book is the story of a yacht, a boyhood dream and a man who walked to both ends of the Earth. Following in the footsteps of Arctic and Antarctic explorers before him, Robert Swan, looked into a crevasse of eternity and then came back to try to tell the world what he had seen.

The yacht *2041* is a vehicle for this message and her historic voyage South with crew members from many different nations out-reaches this story in a spirit of adventure and hope.

The story begins at Sedbergh School in Cumbria when Robert Swan was first inspired by the heroic story of Captain Scott whose deep idealism lives far beyond his icy grave. The boyhood dream to follow "In the Footsteps of Scott" became a practical proposal in 1979 when Robert Swan began to raise the necessary funds.

It took him more than five years to raise the £2.5 million needed. The team, including Captain John Tolson and Dr. Michael Stroud, were based at Cape Evans where Swan was able to visit Captain Scott's hut and its contents, preserved by the intense cold as it was when Scott left on his fateful journey to the Pole. After spending an Antarctic winter in their hut, Swan and his colleagues Roger Mear and Gareth Wood set out to walk 900 miles across the desolate Polar ice cap until, on 11 January 1986, Robert Swan finally achieved his dream and stood at the South geographic pole.

At this moment of achievement, disaster struck. The expedition's ship *The Southern Quest* had been crushed in the pack ice and had sunk. All the crew

Robert Swan, Beardmore Glacier, 1986

were safe but Swan had made a commitment to the expedition's patrons, Sir Peter Scott and Sir Vivian Fuchs that, to show leadership in the conservation of the Antarctic, "Footsteps" would remove their rubbish and equipment from the Antarctic.

This commitment would be delivered on by the team. Three volunteers including Gareth Wood would endure another dark Antarctic winter and the following year the rubbish and equipment was removed by ship but, as ever, the delivery would cost Swan dearly financially - over $500,000 in per-

sonal debts. This financial crisis was added to the disturbing experience of being one of the first people to have walked under the newly discovered hole in the ozone layer.

Following in the footsteps of Scott had been an adventure which left Swan fired by a new idealism - to use his personal experience to tell the world about the environmental problems facing mankind.

In 1987 Swan was awarded the Citation of Merit from the Explorers Club of America. He became a fellow of the Royal

Arrival at the South Pole - Gareth Wood and Robert Swan pull their sledges the final few yards to the American Amundsen-Scott Base.

Pictured right, The Southern Quest going down, crushed by pack-ice closing in on her.

Geographical Society and a council member of the World Wildlife Fund (UK). In December 1988 he was awarded the Polar Medal by HM Queen Elizabeth II for successfully completing the longest unassisted march in history.

The vision now moved north. The Icewalk North Pole expedition, involving 500 sponsors and costing £3.7 million, had a crucial difference. On this expedition 22 young people from fifteen different nations took part in the Icewalk International Student expedition. The students were

Above - Arrival at the North Pole, 14 May 1989, the expedition team led by Robert Swan included Dr. Misha Malakhov, Rupert Summerson, Darryl E. Roberts, Hiro Onishi, Graeme Joy, Arved Fuchs and Angus Kaanerk Cockney.

Pictured left - Members of the Icewalk International Student Expedition

involved in scientific work related to the polar environment.

On 14 May 1989 Swan became the first person to have walked to both North and South poles. He reached the North Pole with eight walkers from seven nations. Again global warming played a part in the expedition with conditions made dangerously difficult by the early break up of the polar ice cap. The ideal behind both Icewalk expeditions was that the environment is an international issue on which nations must work together.

By this time Swan's career as a motivational speaker was firmly established. His experiences of walking nearly 2,000 miles across the most desolate and inhospitable places on the planet gave him an insight into motivation, team work and leadership - all crucial issues to global business.

At the heart of Swan's ethos is the knowledge that people feel helpless when faced with the enormity of global environmental issues. The key is to present the information not as negative, gloom and doom,

Pictured right - The One Step Beyond Expedition 1994 members who all became Special Junior Envoys to UNESCO.

but as positive, achieveable aims. This was the message Swan took to the first Earth Summit in Rio de Janeiro in 1992 where he was a keynote speaker. Two years later he was appointed Special Envoy to the Director General of UNESCO.

Swan said: "Both Sir Peter Scott and Jacques Cousteau asked me, before they died, to try to keep a focus on the preservation of Antarctica. These men had already inspired me and continue to do so. In order to preserve Antarctica we must inspire young people today, especially in the 44 countries who are signatories to the Antarctic Treaty.

"This is why we decided to take 35 young people from 25 nations to Antarctica for the first stage of Mission Antarctica. We took these young people to a place that no one owns and where there have been no wars. We asked them what we should do to help

protect this continent and they chose to remove the rubbish at the Russian Bellingshausen Station.

"These young people will be in their 60s and 70s when the Antarctic Treaty comes up for review in 2041 and we hope they will remember their experience and will act to protect Antarctica."

The themes of youth and positive action for the environment were deeply imbedded in the planning for the 1997 Mission Antarctica expedition. The young people were selected from cultures of

An Elephant seal at Bellingshausen Antarctic Research Station

historical enmity. They included young people from former Yugoslavia - a Bosnian, Croat and a Moslem; an Israeli and a Palestinian, a Russian and a Chechnya, a black and a white South African. The bonds of friendship formed on this expedition may not have prevented bloodshed and war, but six years later the young people are still close friends using e-mail and internet to keep in touch.

Throughout this period, the scientific research continued to pile fact upon fact, leaving little doubt that global warming is happening. Ice shelves, both north and south, are breaking up earlier than ever before and British Antarctic Survey scientists report an increase in mean annual temperature in the region of 4.5 degrees Fahrenheit since the 1940s.

The need to highlight these issues has never been stronger.

Another factor is that, although Antarctica has only been properly explored by mankind in the last century, it has already been threatened by the possibility of exploitation. The Antarctic Treaty, ratified by 44 signatory countries, set up a framework to protect Antarctica from activities such as mining.

The addition of the Environmental Protocol to the Antarctic Treaty added extra force, providing a 50 year protection for Antarctica as the world's last great wilderness. This Environmental Protocol comes up for review in 2041.

Clearly actions speak louder than words. Swan could continue to talk about his experiences but,

Russian engineers funded by Mission Antarctica pictured working at Bellingshausen Antarctic Research Station, emptying old oil from rusty and leaking barrels into new plastic barrels supplied by Mission Antarctica.

given a practical challenge, he could help make a difference and leave the world a better place for our children and our children's children.

The framework for this challenge was Mission Antarctica and the practical task quickly identified was to remove 1000 tons of rubbish from the Russian Research Station at Bellingshausen. This six year programme initially involved sending a team of waste disposal experts who successfully identified and quantified the rubbish.

In following seasons Mission Antarctica, working closely with the Russian government, has paid for Russian engineers to dismantle unused equipment and gather the rubbish on the shore for the final phase when a large ship will visit Bellingshausen to remove the waste which will then be re-cycled.

Clearing rubbish, though a practical, achieveable

and laudable task, does not have immediate media appeal. Swan realised that what was needed was something to act as a symbol of international co-operation, something which would fire the imagination and help focus attention on the need to preserve Antarctica. The idea for a yacht was born to be used as a communications vessel to get the message out to young people in 44 nations.

The Dream

Polar exploration and ships rely on each other like air and fire - you cannot have one thing without the other. Throughout history the great polar explorers relied on their ships - Nansen and *The Fram*, Scott and *The Discovery*, Shackleton and *The Endurance*.

Swan's ship *Southern Quest* was lost, but the dream continued for more than a decade, and was given added meaning by the need to have a vehicle to inspire the dreams of others.

The design and build of a yacht was the first question to address. The yacht had to be capable of sailing in some of the worst seas in the world.

Even more important was the task of raising the funds necessary for such a project. Seasoned by his polar experiences, Swan was ever aware of Scott's famous words: "The most difficult part of any expedition is not the actual journey; it is the planning, the preparation and the fund raising to make that journey possible."

Swan turned to his contacts in The Netherlands and, after months of hard work on budgets, meetings and projected costs, with Johnny Pearson and Alexandra Imholz, the twelve main sponsor companies had generously agreed to "come on board". The vision was clear; the new yacht would be a communications vessel backed by international companies prepared to put the environment firmly on their business agenda.

The search for a yacht of the highest specification led Swan to Plymouth and the famous Challenge Business yachts, designed by David Thomas and built by Devonport Management Ltd. These Bermudan cutter style yachts are built for the

Built for one of the toughest yacht races in the world and designed to the highest specification, the yacht was first launched in 1990 to take part in the Chay Blythe Challenge Round the World yacht race.

world's toughest yacht race - 30,000 miles around the world.

The Challenge yacht race was started by round the world yachtsman, Sir Chay Blyth, CBE, BEM, who was delighted to help Mission Antarctica. The yacht he had in mind already had an impressive history. She was the first ever built for the Challenge Fleet and was launched by Her Royal Highness The Princess Royal in June 1990, who by coincidence, had also visited *Southern Quest* at Tower Bridge in the autumn of 1984.

Sir Chay said: "This yacht holds a special place in my heart. She has been all over the world and has been involved in corporate entertainment, sponsorship and crew volunteer training for all three of our Challenge races to date."

Originally named *Isle of Man*, the 67 foot yacht changed hands for just under £250,000 on 14 May 1999. Significantly this date was ten years to the day after Swan's historic arrival at the North

An historic moment for Robert Swan and for Mission Antarctica - ten years to the day after Swan became the first person in history to walk to both Poles, the contract of sale was signed. The yacht is pictured as she was on that day.

Pole took him into the record books.

It was a moment of sweet achievement to savour deeply, before the hectic round of re-fit work to prepare this racehorse of the seas for a task requiring the strength, safety and stamina necessary to face the notorious weather conditions of the Drake Passage and Antarctica.

The wound left by the sinking of the *Southern Quest* was at last healed. The new yacht was the perfect vessel to focus world attention on the mission to clear rubbish from Antarctica. She had all the elements of adventure, beauty and drama and, what's more, she could take people to see, with their own eyes, this inspirational wilderness. And, for all those people who cannot go to the Antarctic, she would get the message out using the internet.

The Netherlands

One of the first questions to address was the new yacht's name. Ideas came thick and fast until Mission Antarctica expedition leader, Major Bronco Lane, came up with the name *2041*. This was an excellent link back to the yacht's task - to highlight the need to protect Antarctica from exploitation when the Environmental Protocol

2041's maiden voyage for Mission Antarctica took her across the Channel from the UK to Breskens in The Netherlands.

The six man volunteer crew for the voyage were: left to right, back - Robert Swan, Peter Spencer, Paddy Bees. Front - Edward Jongepier, Robert Tan and Adrian Cross.

to the Antarctic Treaty comes up for review in the year 2041.

The urgency of the deadlines of re-fit work in order to get *2041* ready in time to reach Antarctica within the brief window of the southern summer meant there was no time to waste. A few days after the purchase was agreed, *2041* left Plymouth on her maiden voyage for Mission Antarctica.

A crew of volunteers, skippered by experienced Challenge Business yachtsman Paddy Bees, sailed *2041* across the Channel from England to The Netherlands. The crew included Robert Swan, Peter Spencer and Adrian Cross, as well as two Dutchmen, Robert Tan and Edward Jongepier, from Standfast Yachts, the company commissioned to carry out the major re-fit.

Adrian Cross, a previous Mission Antarctica team member, sponsored by Standard Life, described the thrill of that first voyage: "I sit for a moment and think how privileged we are, the six of us. With all this technology under out feet, we are still doing what our ancestors have done over the centuries, as we slide past the historic approaches to Spit Head and Portsmouth. The morning sky now looks like an oil painting and the air has a bite to it. While the world sleeps, we steal along the south coast on our mission."

Once safely at Standfast's yard in Breskens, the work began. One of the advantages of having the re-fit carried out in The Netherlands was that the main sponsor companies could easily travel to Breskens to see how the project was developing.

A Dutch skipper, Rik Witzand, was appointed to manage the *2041* re-fit work, assisted by Vera Dam and Thom van den Berg. They worked extremely

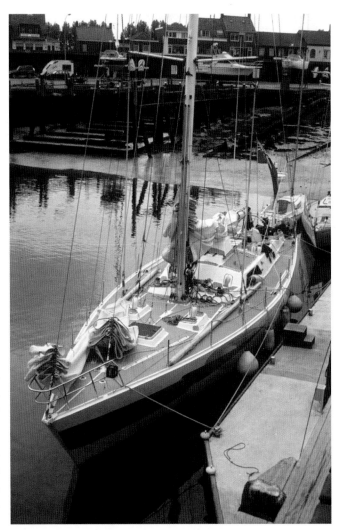

Safely in Breskens Harbour, The Netherlands.

hard to get the work completed. At all times the deadlines were pressing and, as with any large practical project, there were the inevitable set backs.

One of the disadvantages of having the *2041* re-fit work carried out in The Netherlands was that the main Mission Antarctica team were UK based. The

Above Australian Wendy Edwards getting to grips with some woodwork .

London office, on *Mercurius*, a houseboat moored on the Thames, was managed by Annie Holder and Rachel Fleming who could, and did, turn their hands to literally anything, from ordering sails to negotiating insurance deals!

Shortly after the purchase of *2041*, Swan heard a former North Sea fishing trawler, *Seafarer,* was for sale. He decided that, because of the large amount of time team members from the UK would have to spend in Breskens during the re-fit, this sturdy trawler could become a temporary Netherlands base. *Seafarer* was soon moored in Breskens harbour where she served her purpose well, providing office space, a bed for the night and somewhere to meet.

During the summer of 1999 *Seafarer* was home to Australians, Peter Malcolm and husband and wife shipwright team Michael Seeney and Wendy Edwards, all experienced yachtsmen. They worked long hours to help the staff at Standfast and the skipper to complete the re-fit. Both Peter Malcolm and Michael Seeney were trusted and proven men - many years earlier they had been the key to the organisation of *Southern Quest*.

It should not be forgotten that previous team members, such as Mike Hill, played a large part in the background planning and preparation stage which allowed the project to go ahead.

As well as those closely involved with the re-fit, there were many others working hard on behalf of *2041*. Alida Meursing, for instance, who as well as handling the Heerema Group sponsorship, put 100% commitment, on a pro bono basis, into press and PR helping to keep a high profile for the project in the Netherlands media.

The sponsor companies were closely involved too, with many taking a "hands on" approach, going far beyond the call of duty to help get *2041* ready. Keejet Philippens from 1000 Steps acted as a co-ordinator, Unilever gave food supplies for the yacht, Wijsmuller provided extra practical support, Philips helped with electronic equipment and P&O Nedlloyd provided a container for the Russian Bellingshausen project. Above all, Heerema Group went one step beyond with fantastic support across the board.

Meanwhile the selection process for sponsor crew members was in full swing, followed by the essential training and briefing sessions for the mainly novice sailors to prepare for life at sea.

While those involved in the practical work were struggling to meet the deadlines, the media machine was well oiled and had taken on a life of its own. The growing public interest in *2041* was fuelled by the news that HRH The Crown Prince of the Netherlands had agreed to make a personal visit to the yacht in October. This was the first crucial deadline which had to be met.

Daan Westerweel of Wijsmuller took over the management of the yacht refit on behalf of all the sponsors in close conjunction with the captain. He said: "We found that the work was going too slow and it was certain that the visit of Prince Willem Alexander in October and the departure of the yacht in November was not feasible. This meant there was extra time pressure on the whole operation. After analysing all the outstanding jobs, we decided to hire in extra manpower and equipment."

The pressure continued to mount through the heat of the summer until it approached a peak of madness which began to take its toll on everyone. The awful possibility that *2041* would not make it to Antarctica began to creep into the back of people's minds.

Swan bore a great deal of the brunt of the pressure, working incessantly to keep all the pots boiling and acting as trouble shooter whenever it looked like a pot would boil over or needed stirring. His vision kept the team inspired.

2041 in the Standfast Yard, Breskens.

He said: "In the heat of planning, preparation and through all the difficulties, we should never forget why we are doing this. We are working to help the Russians clean up 1000 tons of rubbish from their research station at Bellingshausen and, in the bigger picture, to preserve Antarctica."

The Sponsors

With the support of Neelie Kroes, enthusiasm was mounting for Mission Antarctica in the Netherlands, as multinational companies signed on the dotted line to become sponsors of *2041*.

They saw the positive environmental message as a way of encouraging their employees at all levels to think global and act local. At the same time the *2041* project gave sponsor companies the chance for hands-on involvement in an international environmental mission.

Crew members for the voyage south were to be selected from the major sponsor companies which meant every employee had the opportunity to be chosen to represent their company and work as part of a team sailing *2041* to Antarctica. Although not everyone would have the chance to see the Antarctic, all would play an important part in getting *2041* safely to her destination - every nut and bolt of the re-fit and every mile of the voyage counted.

The reason why the Dutch sponsors were keen to help Mission Antarctica is summed up by Mr. Fred Matser of Miles of Smiles who said: "We chose to participate in Robert Swan's *2041* event, because we share his concern for our planet's serious environmental problems. Robert Swan is dedicated to contributing to the solutions of these problems.

Two of the sponsor crew teams selected - on the left the Philips 2041 crew members and on the right Vopak 2041 crew members.

"Besides that he has an impressive track record dealing with challenging situations in nature more specifically at our two Poles. The combination of these qualities with his media exposure were and still are excellent conditions for a successful *2041* expedition.

"We are happy to be part of it and trust more people will become aware of the responsibility we have in taking care of this planet. We would especially like to thank Mrs. Guusje Hogendoorn for her enthusiasm, time and dedication to help and prepare the trip to Antarctica."

To keep a close financial eye on the sponsor's money Swan approached KPMG the Netherlands to ask them to provide financial expertise that would inspire trust and confidence where the sponsors were concerned. KPMG accepted this request and provided the expertise free of charge. They were assisted in the UK by accountants John Andrew and Ian Coombes.

Henk van der Veen explained: "As a first step we opened an account with Rabobank into which all sponsors could pay their contributions on the basis of cash flows and forecasts about expenditures, the plausibility of plans for the operational period and the refurbishment of the yacht.

"The money could only be released from this account after our authorisation to OSB Expeditions Ltd., or to the wharf directly. We held the most up-to-date version of the forecast. We reviewed the estimates to check their validity and plausibility prior to the initial release of the funds. We also monitored the expenditures throughout the life of the project.

"We frequently met Mr. Swan to discuss the

Henk van der Veen

progress of the project; we had contacts with the office in England and the crew of the yacht. We also visited the wharf at Breskens in the Netherlands where the refit was taking place. There were a number of contacts with the sponsors and we reported to them about the finances.

"We performed this very interesting job with pleasure because KPMG is sympathetic to Mission Antarctica's aim to stimulate awareness of an essential world-wide environmental problem. KPMG also feel that a teamwork based approach is the most effective way for finding solutions.

"It was an honour for KPMG to make its expertise and name available to this project without financial interest and we also offered to assist Robert Swan with future Mission Antarctica projects."

The Prince

The pressure was mounting but, with everyone pulling together, the work at Breskens concentrated on getting *2041* back into the water in time to meet HRH The Crown Prince of the Netherlands.   While *2041* looked fit for a Prince's visit, in fact many jobs had not been properly completed and there had been no time for sea trials.

2041 was lifted gently back into the sea at Breskens and made her way northwards along the Dutch coast to the Royal Maas Yacht Club at Rotterdam for the all important visit.   The sun shone, crowds of people gathered along the harbour walls, the air was charged with excitement.

Last minute details were attended to on *2041* while sponsors, dignitaries including the Mayor of

A gentle lift back into the water and 2041 was at last ready for her voyage to Rotterdam to meet HRH The Prince of Netherlands.

Crowds of excited people waited patiently at the Royal Maas Yacht Club where the sun shone, the band played and a children's choir sang in honour of The Prince.

Rotterdam, team members and a large number of the Dutch press gathered for the Prince's arrival. Swan stood out from the crowd of smart dark suits in a green, rather strangely fitting, English gentleman's suit.

The band played and a group of children sang, looking for all the world like a church choir with their adult-sized Mission Antarctica T-shirts down to their knees. There was champagne, official speeches, photographs, laughter and plenty of informal friendly chatter as the atmosphere relaxed and everyone enjoyed the event. It was also a chance for people from the different sponsor companies to meet. Some of them would be sailing together into the adventure of a lifetime.

The Prince's visit was a milestone and boosted the morale of everyone involved. It was a great achievement; a day to take stock, and realise how far *2041* had come in six months.

Yet, in the back of Swan's mind swelled the memory of storms in the Southern Ocean lashing 50 foot waves at everything in its path. He knew more than anyone what conditions *2041* would meet and he

Above from left to right, Robert Swan, Dutch skipper Rik Witzand and HRH The Crown Prince of the Netherlands.

Left, 2041 pictured in the beautiful surroundings of the Royal Maas Yacht Club, Rotterdam.

Pictured above, 2041's bow showing the UNESCO logo in recognition of Swan's role as Special Envoy to the Director General.

Right, HRH The Crown Prince of the Netherlands leaves 2041 following his morale boosting visit.

Below, the speeches in honour of 2041 and her mission.

was painfully aware of how the window of opportunity provided by the southern summer was already beginning to close.

2041 left Rotterdam for Vlissingen where she was joined by *Seafarer* and the rest of the team so that essential work could continue. The yacht's next appointment at the end of October was fast approaching - she was due to depart for Ijmuiden and then on to London.

On the voyage to Ijmuiden disaster struck. A

Pictured above, some of the team who would help sail 2041 to Antarctica met for the first time at the "christening" event in Rotterdam.

Pictured right, in Vlissingen, the calm before the storm - 2041 and the former North Sea fishing trawler Seafarer, now converted to provide Mission Antarctica's mobile accommodation and office space.

message came through to the UK that *2041* was sinking. It was unimaginable. There are no words to describe that awful moment. Meanwhile Swan was already standing on the quay in Ijmuiden, seemingly unruffled, with the Wijsmuller men. They are salvage experts, so he was in the right company.

In the face of such catastrophe, the only thing to do was to stay calm. So Swan and Dan Westerweel from Wijsmuller, stood and joked on the quay until *2041* finally limped into port and into safe hands.

She was lifted out of the water where the technical problem was isolated. With such a major re-fit and no time for sea trials, it was inevitable there would be adversities to overcome. A prop shaft bearing was replaced and the leak cured.

It seemed that now all would be plain sailing. *2041* would now head for London for a major press conference with invited guests and sponsors from all over the UK, including leader of the opposition, William Haig MP. She would then have a leisurely couple of weeks before finally heading south on her mission.

All the plans had been made, the yacht looking at her best after so much work in The Netherlands. *2041* had been through her trials and tribulations. There was nothing else to hold her back from her voyage south. How wrong we were....

Catastrophe averted, 2041 is saved from a salvage fate by the Wijsmuller salvage men!

UK Crisis

S wan, who was born and brought up near Barnard Castle, County Durham and educated at Sedbergh, Cumbria before Durham University, had long held the ambition to move his operation north. In January 1999 part of this plan had materialised under the management of his old friends, Dawn Robertson and Peter Koronka.

Photographer Peter Koronka took part in the 1999 Mission Antarctica Bellingshausen expedition. Journalist Dawn Robertson, had been involved in Swan's organisation for some time as editor of *Ice Talk* magazine.

The Northern office had been closely involved in the *2041* project throughout and it was natural that they handled the UK press event. The date was booked for 1 November 1999. Meanwhile Annie Holder in London worked long hours on hyper-drive making sure all the details were in place. St. Katharine's Dock in central London was booked as the venue for *2041*'s last port of call before heading south.

Pictured above chief trouble shooter Bronco Lane and left, St. Katharine's Dock event, London - there was no yacht but plenty of people came along to hear Robert Swan speak about 2041 and Antarctica.

Left, Meg Yim who travelled from Hong Kong to become the first 2041 sponsor crew member and right, a short break from crisis management for Annie Holder and Robert Swan.

Confident press releases were sent out to the major UK newspapers and to all the yachting magazines. Invitations to Swan's family, friends and supporters of the *2041* project were sent out for an informal gathering on Sunday 31 October and excitement was intense as this would be the last opportunity to see the yacht and to wish her well. A chance meeting on a train journey, between Swan and the Rt. Hon. William Haig, MP, leader of the opposition had led to his agreeing to visit *2041* on the press day.

Sponsor company Wijsmuller were working closely with Mission Antarctica for the London event and had organised a magnificent buffet, activities for children and an exhibition at St. Katharine's Dock.

The yacht, skippered by her Dutch crew, left the Netherlands slightly behind schedule with the first of the sponsor crew on board. Meg Yim, P&O Nedlloyd, had travelled all the way from Hong Kong for the privilege of being the first to help *2041* on her voyage.

The crew met with bad weather and further technical problems on the crossing from the Netherlands to the UK. She pulled into port in Ramsgate, Kent, too late to continue on up the Thames because the tides were against her.

Bad news travels fast and by 6am on Sunday 31 October, Swan was on the telephone to the Northern office to report the news. Frenetic telephone activity followed, to try and let as many of Swan's family and friends know what had happened. Unfortunately some had already set off on the journey to London where they would meet the Mission Antarctica team and see the exhibition but the Jewel in the Crown, *2041*, would be missing.

The same, slightly less frenetic, telephone calls were made to the press, to sponsors and supporters to warn them of the fact that *2041* was moored in Ramsgate and not London. It was too late to warn some, so the press event went ahead on Monday 1 November.

Swan arrived at St. Katharine's Dock to find *2041*'s berth sadly empty. Thinking on his feet, he and Victor Muller, in order to make up for the disaster of no yacht decided people would have to be entertained so Swan gave four lectures in five hours. Exhausted but never beaten, Swan and his team kept the many visitors happy.

And so the day was saved. The immediate crisis was over but an even larger crisis loomed. The Dutch crew were not happy with *2041*'s condition and were clearly saying that it would be better to delay sailing south for a further year to allow all the technical difficulties to be ironed out.

When in a dark corner, with difficulties and obstacles mounting, it is always good to look for the positive. At this moment in time, with the possibility of the whole project collapsing, the positive light was

Pictured above Peter Milwidsky who took over as 2041 skipper during the UK crisis.

Left - The Berthon Boat Company team who helped with the final work to prepare 2041, left to right: Paul Urquhart, Keith Harris, Pete Belbin, Pete Woodford, Glen Norton, Gary Lancaster, Wendy Edwards (OSB), Simon Baker, Gary Kirk, Dave Bolwell and Den Kitcher.

that at least *2041* was close to home in the UK.

This meant that a crew of willing volunteer pirates were quickly mustered, under the leadership of former SAS Major Bronco Lane, to head for Ramsgate to assess for themselves *2041'*s problems. Bronco

2041 in the Berthon Boat Yard, Lymington.

was joined by Adrian Cross and Peter Spencer as trouble shooters to see how they could help get things organised.

Bronco, who is virtually unflappable, and has a multitude of skills commented that: "It depends how you look at the situation. The cup is either half full or half empty." That summed up the difficulties. It was obvious to Swan and the rest of the team that *2041'*s cup was definitely half full and, by hell or high water, she would be ready to sail south whatever work had to be done.

Everyone found an extra gear they didn't know they had. Volunteers gave their time free to clean up the yacht and do any work which could be done by semi-skilled but willing helpers.

A decision was made to head along the south coast for Lymington and a company called Berthon Boats who were on stand-by to make *2041* their priority task. A list of essential jobs was drawn up and categorised into tasks which required Berthon's technical expertise and those which the volunteers could tackle.

Peter Milwidsky took over the running of the project to co-ordinate the operation and at every possible opportunity Swan joined the team to personally oversee the final works. The cup was getting fuller and fuller.

Confidence was growing and the feeling was, that despite all the setbacks, *2041* would be ready to sail south on the long voyage to the other end of the globe. There was even a glimmer of hope that she might make it to Antarctica before the southern summer finally closed its doors for the long, dark polar winter.

The growing confidence must have been evident because Royal & SunAlliance joined in as the last sponsor for the yacht *2041*. This was a huge boost all round for the project and their timely support helped lift team spirits all round.

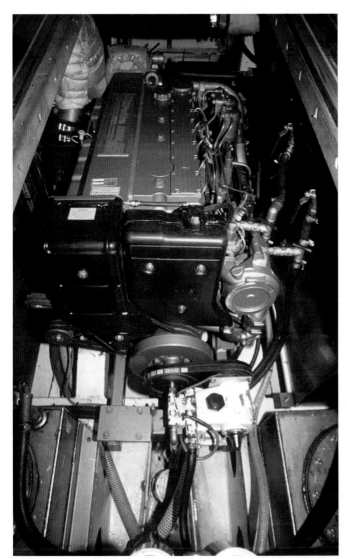

2041's new engine - a Perkins Sabre M185C, 180 horse power turbo diesel propulsion auxiliary.

Captain and Crew

One of the reasons why the re-fit of *2041* was so important was the insistence by Swan that she must meet the highest safety standards. The responsibility for the lives of crew members rested ultimately on his shoulders.

The aim was to achieve a full category 0 unsupported Southern Ocean safety certificate which meant that everything possible had been done to make *2041* safe to meet the challenge of the Drake Passage and Antarctic waters.

Yacht surveyor John Fearnley guided the Mission Antarctica team throughout the long process of preparing *2041* to meet this high standard. In the two weeks before she left Berthon Boat Yard, with a full safety certificate, over 1,000 man hours were put in to get the necessary work completed.

The human strain of working long hours was not the only problem. Swan was all too aware of another aspect of the risk of *2041* not reaching Antarctica in time. There was a careful balancing act - either the yacht failed to go and the whole project collapsed or she went at any price.

The latter decision was the only alternative and all Swan's financial resources were poured into the yacht, leaving the coffers almost bare.

During the time that work continued on *2041* at Lymington, the Dutch skipper, Rik Witzand, along with crew members Vera Dam and Thom van den Berg, decided that they would return to the Netherlands, as their role was complete. Swan recognised how much their fantastic efforts in the Netherlands had contributed to the success of *2041*.

A new crew of experienced Challenge Yacht sailors was appointed. They were headed by 29-year-old Mark Hopking. Born and brought up in Suffolk, on the east coast of England, Mark had been sailing dinghys from a young age. He spent two years working for the John Ridgeway Adventure Centre in Scotland where he gained experience of rough weather sailing.

2041 leaves the Berthon Boat Company, Lymington

Mark has a degree in Recreation and Community Studies from Exeter University and has taken part in numerous yacht races. In the rigorous Fastnet race the yacht Sigmadon he sailed won the Corporate and Top School award.

He has experience as an engineer on a merchant coaster and spent two years as first mate on a 200 foot luxury yacht sailing the Mediterranean and Caribbean. More recently he worked for the Challenge Business, training crews for the BT Global Challenge, as well as taking part in corporate

Pictured above, the new crew, left to right, skipper Mark Hopking, first mate Emily Pearson and engineer Neil Shuttleworth and below, the team, sponsors and friends meet in Lymington.

entertainment for sponsors and adventure sailing.

When he took up the post as skipper of *2041*, Mark said: "I have every confidence in *2041* and am looking forward to this fantastic opportunity to be involved in Mission Antarctica."

First mate, 23-year-old Emily Pearson, comes from Birmingham. Like the skipper, she spent much of her youth "messing about in boats." For the last four years Emily has lived in Southampton, taking part in many yacht races, including the Fastnet. Before she joined *2041* she had completed many Channel crossings and two voyages across the Atlantic.

Working for the Challenge Business, Emily has experience of corporate hospitality and team building. She has a degree in music from Southampton University and, as a flautist, has played with several orchestras. Needless to say, Emily did not leave for Antarctica without her flute.

The third crew member appointed was 39-year-old Neil Shuttleworth from Warwickshire. Neil is an engineering graduate from Sunderland University and, with experience in various engineering backgrounds, had the wide experience necessary to act as *2041* engineer.

The new crew were active in over-seeing the

Pictured left Antarctic historian David Yelverton and above, 2041 shows her style in a photo shoot for Citizen Watches, Japan, of the spinnaker they sponsored.

final work at Berthon Boat yard. In November a sponsor event at Lymington brought sponsors and friends together, as well as providing an opportunity for the new crew to meet other team members.

The highlight at this event was the arrival of Antarctic historian, Mr. David Yelverton, who gave Swan a bottle of vintage champagne, exactly like the champagne taken by Captain Scott to Antarctica almost a century earlier.

Meanwhile, back in London, plans had reached fruition for a final office move to Swan's home area in the North of England. The expedition companies, One Step Beyond and Mission Antarctica, would join 2nd Nature which had been running successfully from an office high on the Pennines.

It was time also for Dawn Robertson and Peter Koronka to move on from their "hands on" role so that they could devote more time to their publishing company while at the same time continuing to provide the "words and pictures" for Swan's organisation.

Adrian Evans

A new manager, Adrian Evans was appointed. Adrian previously worked at Teesside University. Adrian brought managerial skills to his new post as well as a good deal of marketing experience.

Only one last minute task before 2041 finally departed south was left. The yacht had to do some sailing using the spinnaker in order to get some photographs of the sail sponsored by Citizen Watches, Japan. 2041 was put through her paces with the spinnaker aloft, and all seemed to be well. The first sponsor crew arrived in Lymington and, at last, 2041 was ready to head south.

Crisis Management

It was November and *2041* was finally under way.   Or was she? She headed south, out of Lymington, with five crew members from the sponsor companies. These included Seow Ling Teo (Vopak) from Singapore and Jonathan Lewis (P&O Nedlloyd) from New Zealand with the remaining three crew members from the Netherlands - Anne-Marie Janssen (Rabobank), Frans Hogenhout (Wijsmuller) and Wouter Bak (Philips).

As they crossed the Channel, skipper Mark Hopking became increasingly concerned.   There was a strong smell of diesel which made the yacht unpleasant as well as wasting a lot of fuel. The fuel system seemed to be leaking in various places, plus the engine wasn't running smoothly and a lot of water was getting into the bilges.

They were alongside the northern coast of France when Hopking made the decision to return to the UK. The problems were too great to sort out as they sailed and there could be safety implications, a risk he was not willing to take.

Disappointed, they headed back to Plymouth where engineer Neil Shuttleworth set to work on the diesel leaks. It was simply a question of tightening up jubilee clips and replacing some of the lengths of pipe which were too short and pulling enough to

Pictured above left Teo Seow Ling from Vopak, Singapore and right a cold but happy crew off Plymouth.

cause leaks. This problem was quickly cured; others proved harder to resolve.

Mark said: "I had been sailing these boats for two years and it is completely uncharacteristic, and not at all normal, to find water in the bilges. As we sailed back to Plymouth we were all thinking about the cause of this. It seemed the water was coming in down through the deck."

Back in Plymouth the crew found a hole around the anchor windlass. They devised a way of making this water-tight thinking this would cure the problem of water in the bilge.

Twenty-four hours after getting to Plymouth they set out for Las Palmas again but, no sooner had they got to sea, than they discovered that water was still pouring into the bilges and the engine continued to perform poorly. However, there was one piece of good news, at least there were no diesel leaks.

Everyone's patience was being put to the test with the hold-ups particularly difficult for the sponsor crew members who had taken time off work for this once in a lifetime experience. Rumblings of discontent began to sound back in the board rooms of the sponsor companies as bad luck seemed to dog *2041*.

Back in Plymouth, they discovered that the obvious hole near the anchor windlass which they had already filled, was only part of the problem. The anchor windlass itself was not bonded to the deck and water was coming in all around it. In addition two leaks from pipes to the water tanks were found. These problems were soon cured.

The third diffi-

Pictured above Jonathan Lewis from New Zealand and left, 2041 engineer Neil Shuttleworth who tackled a multitude of "teething trouble" tasks before 2041 was finally ready to head south.

culty, with the engine, was not so simple. The crew found that somehow sea water was getting into the engine and into the cylinders, where only fuel and air should mix. Water will not be compressed by the pistons so, once inside the engine the engine failed and would not start.

Various experts, including Peter Malcolm, Mike Seeney and Wendy Edwards hurried to Plymouth to try to sort out what was causing the difficulty with the finger of suspicion firmly pointing to the exhaust system. Various changes were made, but nothing seemed to stop sea water finding its way into the engine.

There was a lot of head scratching and finally, in desperation, the skipper suggested that it might be worth trying moving the exhaust, which was in a different arrangement on *2041* than on a normal Challenge yacht.   It worked! From that point on there were no further problems of sea water getting into the engine.

It had been a monumental struggle to get *2041* sea worthy. There had been no time for proper sea trials and, with the benefit of hindsight, it is obvious that the two false starts would not have hap-

pened if *2041* had undergone proper trials.   As it was, the teething troubles were no greater than could be expected on such a large re-fit.

The skipper had by this time spoken to the crew who hoped to take part in the first leg from Lymington to Las Palmas. They had now had two false starts and Hopking warned that he could not guarantee when *2041* would finally head south - it could be 24 hours or it could be ten days. In addition, even if all the technical problems were solved, he had to consult the weather forecast and this could delay sailing. A disappointed but understanding crew took the decision to return home to be with their families for Christmas.

At such short notice, and with continuing uncertainty as to the departure date, the only sponsor crew members ready to join *2041* for the voyage to Las Palmas were Marty van den Ven, Paul Lugard and Veronique Duivelshof, all from Philips, the Netherlands. To make up the crew numbers, two extra hands were hired - Chris Spencer and Ian Taylor.

This crew were in place by 23 December. They were ready to set off for the third time - all the obstacles in *2041's* path had been

Pictured above Anne-Marie Janssen from Rabobank, Netherlands and below, Wouter Bak from Philips, Netherlands.

cleared. There were no diesel or water leaks and the exhaust system was working perfectly but, with all the major technical problems finally conquered, nature decided to take a hand in the *2041* story.

A vicious south-westerly gale blew up. The wind speed increased until it was 50 knots but, as *2041* was safely moored in the harbour, there should have been no problem. With weather conditions worsening by the minute, the yankee head sail was furled. The drama began when it became obvious the furling gear had somehow failed. Despite every effort the crew could not get the sail down.

A storm brewed in Plymouth

2041 was taking a battering with the sail full of wind which was so strong the yacht and the pontoon to which she was moored were shaking. Finally the inevitable happened and the sail ripped.

Bronco Lane happened to be in Plymouth, as he had travelled with the three crew members from Philips. It was plain that, if the sail could not be mended before Christmas, then it would not be fixed for more than a week as everyone took the seasonal holiday.

After some frantic telephone calls and some generous offers of help, Bronco set off for Hoods Sail Makers in Lymington. Though it was Christmas Eve, the Hoods' staff worked long and hard to mend the sail and, by the end of the day Bronco was heading back to Plymouth with the repaired sail.

Meanwhile the skipper and crew spent Christmas Eve on a final sea trial to check that everything was working properly. Hopking was satisfied the exhaust and engine difficulties were resolved. He confided to Swan that he was "quietly confident" that the yacht would make it to Bellingshausen, but only if there were no further major technical problems. He said: "We just need luck to go our way for a change."

The crew were all far from their homes and families on Christmas Day and had been too busy to organise a Christmas meal on *2041*. Yacht engineer Neil Shuttleworth had some friends who lived just outside Plymouth. He contacted them and in true Christmas spirit, David and Joy, invited the whole crew to spend Christmas with them - an extra eight for dinner!

The festivities were a brief distraction from the main concern - if *2041* did not leave soon it would be too late - she would not get to Antarctica in time. The pressure was enormous, added to which the yacht still had to prove herself after all the work which had been done.

Pictured above skipper Mark Hopking who, despite all the setbacks, confided in Swan that he was "quietly confident" 2041 would make it to Bellingshausen.

Finally on 27 December, *2041* headed out of Plymouth, leaving the UK for the third time. This was definitely it. All the delays, the dilemmas, the doubts, everything that had happened had held 2041 back until this moment, which was the right time for her to set sail.

If the team had tried to organise this it would not have happened. Fate had stepped in to play its part in the story of *2041*. All the clutter of thoughts and worries, the constant activity, the plans and details had drawn a veil over the very reason why *2041's* journey was so important. It was easy to lose sight of this, but then suddenly brought into focus was the fast approaching historic moment as the world entered a new Millennium.

Having a perspective on those last days in December 1999, it could not have been a better time for *2041* to set out on her journey south, than the closing minutes of the 20th century. She was created, planned and prepared, in the 20th century for a voyage which held out hope for environmental change in the 21st century.

Heading South

2041 slipped quietly out of Plymouth at 2.30pm on 27 December. There was no big send off, no crowds on the quay side, no cheering or photographs. The time for celebrations had passed and, with so many false starts and set backs, nobody could believe that the voyage had really begun. It seemed likely that *2041* would be back in the UK soon.

The crew were filled with a quiet determination. It was time for action and, as they motored away in perfect weather conditions, and then hoisted the mainsail, Hopking's confidence in *2041* began to grow. Instead of worrying about the yacht, he was now concerned about the weather forecast - a force 11 gale in the Bay of Biscay - right in *2041*'s path.

Rather than head for the eye of the storm, Hopking steered a course along the south coast for Falmouth, 45 miles away. The crew were disappointed not to be heading straight south, but relieved that they would spend a calm night in Falmouth, rather than a stormy one at sea.

On board *2041* apart from the main crew were Veronique Duivelshof, Marty van den Ven and Paul Lugard, all from Philips in the Netherlands, plus Chris Spencer and Ian Taylor who provided extra muscle power for this first leg of the voyage.

The following day the news from the Bay of Biscay confirmed that the skipper had made the right decision with numerous ships and tankers in the area suffering damage from the heavy seas. The forecast was now good, with sunshine, light winds and so, hoisting the sail, winching the winches and

Captain's Log:
Plymouth - Las Palmas
Depart - 27/12/99
Arrive - 7/1/00
Distance -1537nm
Estimated time - 10 days
Actual time - 10 days
Average speed - 6.4kn

As the second Millennium drew to a close and the third Millennium began, 2041 was at last heading south on her historic journey.

coiling the ropes the crew finally turned *2041*'s bow southwards.

As they headed out to sea the first signs of sea-sickness appeared with Veronique heading for her bunk but she soon came back on deck when she heard dolphins were swimming alongside *2041*, like a guard of honour, accompanying *2041* out into the ocean. Good fortune was at last smiling on *2041* and her crew; the journey had really begun.

The last hours of the 20th century were drawing to a close as Paul Lugard wrote: "We are making good progress and have crossed a remarkably calm Bay of Biscay and are now somewhere east of northern Spain. Both the big sail, the yankee and the staysail are out. Our speed is eight knots with fifteen knots of wind....Now that the adjustments of the first few days have been shaken off, there are plenty of moments of pure bliss."

The watch system was running smoothly and the crew even had time to turn their attention to the finer things in life - like sorting out a music system so those in the doghouse could enjoy a varied selection from modern dance to classical.

The dolphins danced in the waves alongside the yacht and the weather continued to be perfect. On board morale was high, with good team spirits and time for quiet reflection on the bigger picture in which they were all playing their part.

Celebrating the New Millennium on board *2041* was a very special moment. The style was a little odd, but the sentiments were of the best, as the crew dined on Fray Bentos pies washed down with champagne, followed by music and dancing on deck.

The skipper donned a silly dinosaur hat and Marty

At the helm, Veronique Duivelshof from Philips, Netherlands.

could not resist the sea any longer and dived in to swim in the perfectly calm water. He explained that there is a tradition in the Netherlands of a New Year's dive into the North Sea. The sea off Spain was somewhat warmer than the North Sea but only Marty was brave enough to keep up the tradition.

Marty's chance for a second swim came sooner than expected when it was discovered that some netting was dragging from one of the anodes under the hull and had to be freed by hand.

2041 was in a ridge of high pressure which was moving south with the yacht and winds were so slight that the crew were forced to motor. The skipper reported: "The boat is coming up to speed thanks to a lot of elbow grease from all of the crew. We are all starting to take pride in *2041* and look forward to showing her off in Las Palmas."

The weather had been kinder than could be expected as they crossed the Bay of Biscay and all the crew were now completely recovered from any seasickness. Food consumption doubled - at one meal Veronique made 41 pancakes - more than five each!   Everyone had settled into the routine and spirits rose even further - it was time for the skipper to start them on their team projects. The philosophy behind these tasks was that each sponsor crew would undertake a project which would make *2041* safer and easier to use for future crews.   The projects included things like making a plan of the fresh water system, noting all the safety equipment on board as well as more practical tasks such as applying anti-slip surfaces on parts of the deck.

Celebrating New Year's Eve, left to right, back - Paul Lugard, Mark Hopking, Neil Shuttleworth and front - Veronique Duivelshof, Jan, Chris and Marty van den Ven.

Throughout the journey from the UK to Las Palmas, the crew continued to improve the yacht's systems while Hopking kept a close eye on everything in case of any potential problems. He kept a very close eye on the weather too and was in frequent communication with "Herb". The skipper explained: "I speak to Herb, the Guru of weather routing for cruising yachtsmen, on a regular basis. I have used him before and find him quite remarkable. He does it for a hobby and has ended up playing both a vital part in the safety of cruising yachts-men in the North Atlantic and a focal point for each day. Through Herb we discovered that the storm we avoided in the Bay of Biscay turned out to be the storm of the century with winds of between 80 and 100 knots, which is a tad breezy. We are very glad we delayed our departure."

Marty, writing on 2 January, said: "It was a very nice celebration of the Millennium with the elements. Only we need a little more of the element wind. We crossed the Bay of Biscay and it was as flat as a mirror. "

Soon the wind did pick up a little and they were able to hoist the spinnaker which, with a force three or four wind, carried them along for a whole after-

Marty van de Ven from Philips, Netherlands, (left) who kept up the Dutch tradition of a New Year dip and Ian. Here they are pictured helping out with the extreme helming experience!

noon until the wind increased so much that they poled out the yankee and the crew enjoyed some extreme helming.

During this period Veronique took the decision, after consultation with Philips, that she would carry on with *2041* to make the Atlantic crossing. She and Emily were sitting on deck when Chris and Ian said they had spotted some dolphins swimming in the opposite direction - to sailors this means bad luck.

Veronique wrote: "I cannot possibly think that something bad will happen....everything is like a dream and too good to be true." The conversation had been about how it was very difficult to make the skipper loose his temper.

The dolphins, the conversation - they were tempting fate and next day somehow a cup of coffee was spilled inside the laptop. The computer refused to work and the accident meant there were no more e-mail messages until the crew could replace the machine in Las Palmas.

By this stage of the journey it was becoming more and more difficult to cook interesting meals. The supply of fresh meat and vegetables was exhausted but the cupboards were still full of sausages and noodles so culinary imagination became an important talent.

On 6 January *2041* was getting very close to Las Palmas and at last the wind picked up enough for some real, prolonged sailing. Veronique wrote in her diary: "The ocean is really getting rough. The engine is switched off and the sails are up: we are sailing! After the tedious motoring we are all excited. This is the best way we could end our journey."

With Grand Canaria in sight, Marty, Paul, Ian and Veronique hooked themselves onto their lifelines and went out to play on the foredeck. The object of the game was to walk, with very shaky legs, to the very front of the boat and wait for a huge wave to almost wash them away. It was exhilarating, exhausting and seriously good fun.

By 8.30 in the evening *2041* was in the harbour, with all the lights of the island glittering around her. The whole team were tired, hungry and filled with a sense of achievement that they had made it. *2041*

2041 arriving in Las Palmas

plenty to eat and drink and a chance to relax for a few hours.

The first stage was over but there was no time for complacency. The skipper said: "We still have a very long way to go and very little time to do it. I cannot commit to getting to Antarctica yet, but we are revved up for the challenge."

With her huge sponsor flags hoisted up the forestay, *2041* could not be missed and many people curious about the boat came along to ask where she was going and what she was doing. The mission had really begun.

was one step closer to her final destination - Antarctica.

There was not long to reflect on the success of this first leg of *2041*'s journey. After a good night's sleep the crew were back at work tackling the many tasks which were easier to do while in port. There were technical issues like improving the auto-pilot and many handyman jobs such as fixing cupboards.

The crew for the Atlantic crossing arrived during the morning while Marty, Paul, Chris and Ian headed for home. Swan arrived with an American colleague, Guy Courtney, and they also were quickly involved in the tasks which had to be done to get *2041* back to sea as quickly as possible.

Veronique tackled the shopping list which included everything from onions to a chart of Salvador harbour. Gas bottles had to be re-filled and the yacht re-fuelled. There was laundry to do and the crew all managed to have a good wash as well as

Extreme helming livens up any voyage!

Atlantic Crossing

The crew who met in Las Palmas ready for the 2,600 nautical mile Atlantic crossing included three Vopak representatives - Hans Stigter and Hans de Willigen from the Netherlands and Eric Strautins from Australia. They were joined by two further Dutch people - Veronique Duivelshof from Philips and Tom Wain from P&O Nedlloyd.

Seasickness took its toll not long after *2041* left Las Palmas on 9 January and the skipper found the experience and enthusiasm of Hans de Willigen was a great help until the rest of the crew found their sea legs.

As the yacht drew away from land Tom Wain wrote how small and insignificant he began to feel in the face of the Atlantic. As he took over his first watch the only sign of civilisation outside the yacht was a tiny glow in the sky from Gran Canaria. In the sky above a new moon had risen and the heavens were filled with an amazing display of stars while in the sea below the plankton were phosphorescing as *2041* cut through the waves.

Mesmerised by the new experiences Tom was filled with tranquillity until he heard a sound like someone coughing close by. This was impossible as the yacht was already miles out to sea. He turned and there, leaping out of the dark water alongside the yacht was a dolphin. There were several more, their light colour and the sparkling trail they left in the water making it possible to see them, even though it was dark.

In the middle of the Atlantic there was nothing but water and sky in a perfect circle all around the yacht.

The Atlantic crew: back row - Mark Hopking, Hans de Willigen (Vopak), Tom Wain (P&O Nedlloyd) Robert Swan, Hans Stigter (Vopak), Emily Pearson (First Mate), Eric Strautins (Vopak), Veronique Duivelshof, (Philips) and Neil Shuttleworth

Eric Strautins wrote: "The perspective of the immense size of the ocean! With a twenty mile horizon we see 1,200 square miles at each scan. 8,000 square (nautical!) miles a day. On average we've seen a

Captain's Log:
Las Palmas - Recife
Depart - 9/1/00
Arrive - 24/1/00
Distance - 2606nm
Estimated time - 20 days
Actual time - 15 days
Average speed - 7.2kn

ship or another yacht once every two days, or 16,000 square miles."

There was however a strict routine on board which kept this tiny speck moving ever closer to her goal. Hans Stigter explains the intricacies of the watch system and the feeling of being alone on an immense ocean: "On board we are working with a two watch system. Each shift does three watches a day. In the day there is a watch starting at 6am, and in the evening and night-time we do two watches each of four hours. Between them we do some cleaning work, and also the cooking. We make two hot meals a day. With the watch system we're going to our bunk three times a day for two or three hours. So you will understand that after a few days we don't know what day it is anymore...

"Helming at night when we're lucky the moon is bright and thousands of stars are shining, an incredible view. In the darkness you feel the wind, swells and *2041* is better than ever a wonderful feeling. Time to think things over...."

For most of the crossing *2041* raced before north easterly trade winds averaging nearly 200 miles a day meaning that the yacht was well within schedule.

The skipper wrote: "We keep getting forecasts of decreasing wind but they never seem to quite get to us as we race on south. The temperature on the yacht is certainly warming up now and people for the first time are beginning to take cold showers. The sea temperature is in the mid twenties. We are under constant attack from flights of kamikaze flying fish. The debris on deck in the morning is quite a sight."

The best thing of all was that the yacht was literally flying along and at this rate she would certainly reach Ushuaia in time and, for the first time the captain allowed himself to think that they might make it. This was still a private thought as Hopking knew all too well how in this region they could at any moment be gripped by the lethargy of the doldrums.

However, as they approached the Equator the doldrums they feared still did not materialise. This was some consolation for the over-powering heat. It was 30 degrees by mid-day with the ocean a mere three degrees cooler and the humidity very high. Temperatures fell very little at night and the crew found sleeping difficult.

Hans Stigter on duty in the galley.

Tom said: "The idea of sleeping has become almost fantasy. During the day when we are off shift and the sun is beating down on this steel boat of ours you break into a hideous sweat just thinking of going below out of the wind. At night when the sun stops beating down the boat cools but the air maintains its temperature and a lot of condensation forms within the boat making the humidity worse and the atmosphere incredibly sticky."

Cooking too was difficult as Veronique explains: "Cooking below decks in this heat is a slow and breathtaking process. A simple meal will take at least twice as long to prepare as at home. The galley is rather small so being thrown from one side to the other is aside from being painful not that bad. The difficulty is to open a cupboard at the right time: wait for the right wave, open the cupboard very quickly, take out what you want and close it very quickly before the boat leans over the other side and the entire contents fly out. Bad timing (or waves) may also cause the cupboard to close while your hand is in it.

"Cutting vegetables is not too hard, you just have to stop them rolling away.   We have to wear our waterproof sailing trousers when cooking. This is a strict rule because only your waterproofs will protect you from the boiling water and hot food that can easily be spilled under these bumpy circumstances."

As the yacht approached the Equator Hans de Willigen recorded the feeling of nerves the crew felt as they approached this turning point between northern and southern hemispheres: "The tension of the yacht's crew can be felt everywhere. What will King Neptune think, what will happen to the crew? For all of us this will be the first time to pass this

mile stone in yachting. What does the southern hemisphere look like, won't we fall off the globe, will the sun indeed go from east via north to the west? This will all be cleared after tomorrow, and yes we do look forward to it!

"While being at the wheel at night and thinking, it becomes even more clear to me that the whole population should be able to find at least a stable way of living on this planet. The co-operation of us, the flora and fauna and the various areas on the globe is the key and respect for your environment. The goal

Hans de Willigen, also known as Hans the Hooligan, doing a spot of Atlantic pole dipping.

of this Mission Antarctica therefore is a good example in this respect. The Antarctic area is of such a great importance in terms of the animal food chain, the global weather and the global fresh water supply. Antarctica must be kept after 2041 an untouched place."

On 20 January *2041* reached the Equator and finally hit the doldrums. Eric reported: "So after feeling the yacht cut through the water like a long sharp knife all day, evening came. Herb's radio forecast suggested fast moving, equatorial squalls and we could see them around the horizon. Thick heavy clouds, occasional rumbles or flashes of lightning. A few baby squalls, just small low black clouds, went overhead with just a few gusts - quite fun to ride a couple of minutes of 18-20 knots with the light spinnaker up!

"Then at 2:20am this morning the whole eastern sky suddenly became tumbling black. All clearly visible with a near full moon. "Mark!" we shouted. The moon went out and it was dark. With precision that we normally lack, the five of us are in place. Helm. Sheet. Clew. Halyard. Foredeck. Foredeck light blindlingly switched on. The spinnaker is soon safely down and stowed. A few minutes later as the winds are still low, the usual Yankee and Stay foresails are up.

"Then......then nothing. The sea holds its breath. All is quiet. The moon comes back out. The first time in 2,000 miles we had no real boat speed. Becalmed."

The skipper describes that night: "Last night we had the mps up until about 03:00 when a black cloud came over the horizon and we opted to take it down, just in case. Up until that moment it had been almost

Tom Wain was the only crew member who had ever crossed the Equator before.

like daylight on deck with the near full moon. With this cloud came not wind but torrential rain and amazing lightning. We turned all the instruments and communication systems off just in case we got struck and blew all of them in one go. Six hours later and we have just put them back on again. This has meant that the helmsmen have had no more than the compass to steer with.

"The rain is still with us and looks set in for a while and so we may be crossing the equator under thick cloud and rain! It is still very hot though and

All of 2041's crew faced charges when King Neptune held his Equator court.

rain is not such a bad thing in these latitudes. With the rain came the calms that we have been waiting for and so now have the motor on and we are chugging in the direction of the equator. It has been ten days since leaving Las Palmas and this is the first time we have had the engine on. With luck we will be sailing again soon."

Eric continues the story as the yacht grew ever closer to the Equator: "The Doldrums had arrived. A little later the engine was started and we began motoring. This morning when I awoke for my 7am

watch everything and everyone is wet. 'Oh you should have seen the rain. Like pouring from buckets.' Yeah, my watch also had its share. Close grey rain in every direction. No features. Disorienting. While motoring we watched the wind vane resemble a roulette wheel - the wind light and rolling around all compass points!

"And the sea, still now as the moon rises tonight. The sea is disorienting too. This area is truly in convergence. A one to two metre north easterly swell is mixing with a one metre south easterly swell. Cancelling waves smaller, reinforcing waves higher. At times too the surface is oily smooth - yes, I've read about this, it actually looks viscous like oil not water. All silent. Eerie. Expectant.....Expectant.

"We are rather worried about the heavy dark clouds that seem always on the horizon while our weather has improved to a near clear, mild - only a slightly less sweltering 28 degrees, lovely afternoon. Was it some uncertainty about the impending Equator crossing? I'm from Australia but have never crossed the Equator at sea. Everybody else has never been to the Southern Hemisphere. Would King Neptune soon appear and require sanctifications, sacrifices, what?

"At 5pm all were called onto deck by a strange blue covered authority - 'King Neptune's court will soon be in session.' When all were humbly seated, King Neptune appeared like a vision, resplendent in a white robe to match his long beard, with silver head-dress and trident. 'King Neptune's court is now in session. At 30 degrees West on this Equator you are charged...."

"And so began the humility of each of us, including the skipper and engineer Neil when they mysteriously reappeared later after the King and Clerk magically vanished, being baptised on the head from a bucket of kitchen slops, garlic, cat food and rank sauces."

"We were charged as follows:

- myself for hour glassing the spinnaker, loosing a bucket overboard and polluting the sea with a vegetable garden otherwise known as the contents of my stomach when I was seasick last week;

- Hans de Willigen for cruelly cooking with too many potatoes and garlic cloves, and especially for appearing well groomed and neatly attired each morning (when the rest of us looked feral);

- Veronique for her accidental gybe, cooking too many pancakes and for "bringing Philips lighting to an ocean where moonlight is already perfect;"

- Tom for hogging the helm when there's work to be done and for cooking sausage, baked beans and instant mashed potatoes for Sunday Lunch (proudly English!);

- Hans Stigter for wavering under the call of his tearful children calling "Daddy don't go!" and, disoriented this morning in the rainstorm with most

Summary justice for Eric Strautins, Vopak.

instruments turned off in case of lightning, motoring 120 degrees off course!

- Emily for sleeping when off-duty! using tomato sauce on every meal and keeping a waif-like figure while consuming every food additive known to man;

- Neil for running the diesel generator during afternoon Siesta, for owning the most disgustingly smelly old running shoes and sporting an unkempt beard. Neil subsequently threw the shoes overboard and shaved clean for the first time in 18 years!

- and, Mark, for not sharing his sour mix candies with the crew despite being re-supplied by Robert Swan himself in Las Palmas!

Mark then called, "Who's navigating? What's our position?" The GPS was duly read. We motored

The Equator!

Above - following King Neptune's harsh justice the crew were ordered overboard to swim across the Equator!

Right - a warm and enthusiastic welcome awaited 2041 in Recife where the Brazilian press turned out in force to hear about Mission Antarctica.

south about 500 metres, turned off the engine and Mark announced that we all must SWIM over the Equator. It was to be a first for *2041* too, as she had never been into the southern hemisphere before.

"All, except one safety person who was left on board, variously jumped, dived and somersaulted into the clearest sapphire blue. No fear of striking the bottom 3,500 metres below! We swam under the boat, took photos and videos finally climbing back on board to sip warm champagne to celebrate our achievement: To have crossed half the world by nature's breeze. To have swum in the middle of the sapphire ocean. All the while gently becalmed.

"Everyone of us happy with each other and ourselves and the boat that brought us here. Certainly the most satisfying trip of a lifetime! And all the while *2041* is steaming toward her great Antarctic

Mission!"

Reflecting on the voyage Eric said: "I still remain surprised at the various motivations of the various participants here. Holiday, adventure, mission. But a general natural goodness. A few idealists. We haven't talked about it amongst the group for a few days now, having earlier discovered big gulfs.

"We are, though, and despite working as we go, passengers. As the journey's end comes into range, our thoughts are dividing us again into our individual returns to ordinary work and affairs.

"So what have we learned or achieved? We're succeeding in the timely delivery of *2041* for her important mission in Antarctica this season! Individually we've learned some sailing, about the ocean and her fishes. Have we been changed by the experience? Each individual must reply.

"I'm feeling stronger about my existing personal commitments to the environment and the world through the Australian Conservation Foundation, Bushcare and Oxfam. Clear too in the practical work attitude to the environment at Vopak. But I'm also looking forward to helping Robert Swan's leadership activities into the future where I can.

"I feel firstly that I owe him the sincerest thanks for my berth on *2041's* inaugural trip. Thanks also to Vopak's Carol van den Driest's sponsorship too! I also believe in Swan's internationalist, next generation visions and am keen to support his useful, environmental direct actions."

"A voyage in the wild ocean, towards an Antarctic wilderness. It's brought me closer to the natural world. I've sailed the vast Atlantic Ocean in a small boat. I belong to the natural world. The ocean let me pass and didn't smash any of us dead - though it well could have! How comforting, in this age of technical medical advances, high road and crime death rates, to be threatened only by nature! And tiny as I am, I feel the peace and privilege of this closer connection to the natural planet. This I will bring home!"

In the early hours of 24 January *2041* arrived safely in Recife where skipper Mark found the Brazilian bureaucracy formidable. In contrast to the difficult paperwork, the Brazilian welcome was warm with enthusiastic interest from the press.

Despite his gruelling schedule, Swan was at every port of call to meet *2041*, to inspire and support the crew. The message had to be positive to keep up morale and keep the yacht racing south before the southern winter. At the same time, Swan was grappling with the mammoth task left by the financial consequences of pouring all resources into *2041*.

South American Coast

The race was now officially on. *2041* had made up so much time on the first two legs that the goal was now officially a possibility. Relaxing though was out of the question as there were still 3,609 nautical miles to go to Ushuaia.

The crew who sailed *2041* out of Recife at the end of January included Leonore Baljon and Robin Ralling from Vopak, Benny Beek and Carla Stiekema from Rabobank, Netherlands, Frans Hogenhout from Wijsmuller, Vincent Peeters from P&O Nedlloyd and Huub Ehlhardt from Philips.

The press reception and send off at

Above, a stark reminder of the mission for the new crew - pollution in Recife harbour - the glue sniffing kids swim in this water.

Left Carla Stiekema from Rabobank, Netherlands.

Captain's Log:
Recife - Mar del Plata
Depart - 29/1/00
Arrive - 12/2//00
Distance - 2349nm
Estimated time - 16 days
Actual time - 14 days
Average speed - 6.9kn

Recife had been nothing less than spectacular as Carla recorded: "We were filmed by a TV crew while we were working on the jobs list or cooling in the shade. The following day some people came to the yacht who had seen us on TV. That was quite impressive."

Skipper Mark wrote: "While we are heading south with the steamy Brazilian coast just over the starboard horizon I read the reports coming from the team in Antarctica. The gap between us is still thousands of miles but closes with every wave that we pass. While we sip pineapple juice, they hug mugs of tea and hot chocolate to keep warm. While we watch for the next flying fish they watch for icebergs. It is amazing that soon we will be in the colder climates of the far south."

Similar thoughts of the mysterious frozen continent ahead were going through Frans' mind as he wrote: "All alone in the Southern Atlantic, approximately near Cabo de Santa Marta Grande 300 nautical miles offshore the Brazilian coast. Sitting on deck in short trousers it's weird to think about the reasonable possibility that this boat will be completely covered with ice within one month.

"Since leaving Recife anything could have happened in the world without us knowing it. I don't really care but it is very different from what we are used to at home in this time of easy accessible information sources."

It was strange to think of the ice ahead when the crew were sweltering in tropical heat. The skipper described it as being in a 67 foot tin box being roasted for 18 hours a day.

The sailing routine was quickly set as Huub records: "The sponsor crew is now getting used to life on board. The mantra of the watches dictates the daily routines. The crew is divided into two groups. One headed by Emily, the other (mine) by Neil. Captain Mark is on "24-hour-duty". The watches are alternating. One day my group will start with the morning watch, the next day the other group will."

Though the routine was the same, each leg of *2041's* voyage was an adventure in itself. As they made their way down the South American coast, the fact that the Antarctic summer was now past its peak began to loom large. It was a race to get south before winter's door finally closed.

This leg of the voyage was not blessed with such favourable winds and often they had to motor with the added difficulty of avoiding a major seismic survey being carried out in the ocean off

Pictured above Benny Beek from Rabobank, Netherlands

and below Huub Ehlhardt from Philips, Netherlands

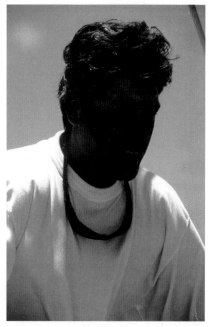

Pictured right Vincent Peeters from P&O Nedlloyd

and below Frans Hogenhout from Wijsmuller, the Netherlands

the South American coast, with ships dragging cables up to five miles behind them.

Vincent wrote: "The deadline is clear, to be in Ushuaia before the ice is too far north and the way to Bellingshausen is cut off. This means we have a schedule to make, and motoring from time to time is unavoidable when the wind lets us down. And the wind lets us down frequently. All kind of tricks have been taken to keep us sailing, including hoisting the spinnaker, poles for the Yankee in various positions etc., but this resulted only in a lot of sweat dripping on the deck but no more progress in speed.

"For the last two days we sailed through various active seismic survey areas. These areas are as big as my home province of Utrecht and we managed with our course and speed to interfere with them all.

This resulted in a lot of sail changes to keep enough distance from their tows."

The yacht, the ocean and the mission brought out the poet in Robin who wrote: "Mere words are unable to express the emotions I feel at the honour I have been given. A chance to steer a tall ship, in the rolling South Atlantic swell, using only the Southern Cross as my mark. And as the night watch passes, the bright clear light of the last of the crescent moon drags the peach veil of the pre-dawn sky upwards....

"These are dangerous, heady drugs, and should only be used by the hard-hearted. My soul is lifted, and I seek no other mere Earthly pleasure. I choke, and tears roll down my hoary old cheeks: I am at one with my heritage, an Englishman in an expedition to far away lands, using only the forces of God's creation, and their skills and courage to win through against the elements, and the dark forces opposing them."

In less poetic mood Robin explained how the experience helped build a team from a group of strangers. At one point a sheet rope parted and a sail broke free. Within seconds Mark and Emily

were on the scene to help but, when it came to retrieving the broken sheet, Robin volunteered to climb the fore-stay.   He realised: "My life was in Frans' hands, as he hauled me up the wildly swaying rigging; his in turn was dependent on Leonore maintaining control of the vessel's steering with only the reefed main up, in difficult conditions. Overseeing all was Emily, watch leader, and experienced, though barely into her twenties, in this sort of sailing and running repair."

Sailing brought out the best in Leonore who wrote: "The sailing is absolutely great. When I am at the wheel I feel like I am flying. We lost sight of all land during the first night on board. After we got rid of a lobster pot holding us back. There is only sea everywhere you look and we saw dolphins. They were playing by the bow. This was the happiest thing I ever saw. What lovely, lively creatures.

"We have been in an area for days now where you must be careful for there might be rockets! It all looks so peaceful out here that this is hard to believe. Here we are in a world that is even more beautiful than I ever knew, and someone is testing rockets. And we are on our way to the last wilderness on earth where there is lots of garbage to clean up."

As well as the dolphins, the crew were to see flying fish, an albatross, Atlantic petrels and most amazing of all whales. The dolphins had followed the yacht for hundreds of miles and, as they approached Mar del Plata, they again came to *2041* and it seemed to the crew they were saying farewell.

As they neared Mar del Plata the connection with Herb in Canada, who had provided so much help with navigation, grew fainter. Mark noted: "We are

Pictured above Leonore Baljon from Vopak, Netherlands, doing her favourite job - helming.

Right Robin Ralling from Vopak, UK.

still just picking up Herb up in Canada and he is helping us with the routing. It is a shame but I fear that we will not be able to keep our relationship going for much more as the distance between us grows every day."

On arriving in Mar del Plata on 12 February Benny, a 50-year-old "green" banker who had never flown or sailed before, wrote: "We made it. We only saw water for days and days....We now know the answer on how to sail an ocean; take only one wave at a time, and take it as a team....

It rained as 2041 reached Mar del Plata but, within half an hour, the rain stopped and the crew were welcomed by the most beautiful sunset. The structure in the picture is a grain silo.

"Our part in Mission Antarctica is only just beginning. Back at the office we need to spread the word on environmental issues. In our home countries we need to keep Mission Antarctica alive with children. We will. This trip brought us closer to nature. We now know how beautiful the world is and therefore we are motivated to preserve her."

Only six weeks before *2041* and the whole project had been shrouded in doubt. Now in the heat of the tropics, the clouds evaporated. The aim was clear and it was possible. In the sticky heat, Hopking was focusing on getting ice reports. Already the ice was moving north but, there was still time, given favourable winds and good fortune.

Tierra del Fuego

The final leg south, before the crossing to Antarctica, took the team from Mar del Plata down to Ushuaia, the southern-most town in the world at the very tip of South America. Taking part on the voyage were two men from America - Gorden Clute, P&O Nedlloyd and James Ferguson, Vopak.

The remaining team members were from the Netherlands and included Saskia Blom from Philips, Willem Ganzinga from Wijsmuller, Paul Spaans and Matty Hakvoort, both from One Thousand Steps and finally Jan Rudolf Westerveld from Rabobank.

This crew had the most previous sailing experience and this helped enormously as they all quickly found their sea legs and settled into a routine. Willem describes the team he found himself a part of: "So far I found that we have a commercial man, an operational man, a financial advisor, a psychiatrist, a research woman and a naval architect. They all have been pecked by the same penguin and are crazy about sailing.

"Some have just started thinking about the environment, on a personal basis as well as on a world wide basis, while others were already busy with this subject. This mission has made us all re-think this aspect of life. At least this group of people will try to be more environmentally friendly and start making more people (especially friends and colleagues) aware of their way of using natural resources and creating waste. We have started a brain storm session that may take some days, but should result in an action plan to make more people aware of what's going on with

Captain's Log:
Mar del Plata - Ushuaia
Depart - 20/2/00
Arrive - 28/2//00
Distance - 1260nm
Estimated time - 10 days
Actual time - 8 days
Average speed - 6.5kn

Pictured left Jan Rudolf Westerveld from Rabobank, the Netherlands, who kept the crew amused with his sailor's songs and below, Jamie Ferguson from Vopak, USA.

Pictured above Saskia Blom from Philips Research, the Netherlands - calm and collected at the helm.

Left, Paul Spaans from One Thousand Steps, the Netherlands whose skills in the galley were particularly appreciated.

respect to Antarctica as well as our world of which we have only one."

As *2041* left Mar del Plata on 20 February Jan wrote: "Finally we can continue on this great quest. We'll be bringing this ship south, where Ushuaia will be the springboard for the final leg to Bellingshausen. Weather has been pretty good from the moment we cast off. There has been little cloud cover, and temperatures have been good.

"We experienced a terrific night. The moon was full and all around us the ocean was lit in a milky sort of light. Last night we encountered a group of about a dozen dolphins. It's a great sight watching them play in the waves at the bow."

On the last leg the yacht had averaged 165nm a day with an average speed of around seven knots. This leg down the South American coast was some 1300 miles but skipper Mark was expecting to encounter head winds to hamper their progress.

He said: "The strategy for this leg is to hug the coast of South America in order to try to pick up the southbound counter current that flows against the general flow of the Falkland Island Current. This will also allow us the opportunity to make the most of the likely winds we expect to encounter."

From the half way point of their voyage, Willem wrote: "Finally last night we had our first taste of the Southern Ocean winds at 40kts across the deck, heavy seas, and the sea temperature dropping rapidly, down to 13 degrees Celsius.

"Hoping not to "taste" much more of the Southern Ocean, we are now heading for the more favourable current, and smoother seas of Bahia Grande (very close to Straits of Magellan).

Surprisingly as the conditions have become more rigorous, *2041's* performance improves, a characteristic I have never experienced on prior yachts.

"After discussing this with the full time crew members I now know why: *2041* has been specifically designed for the round the world BT Challenge Yacht Race - 14 identical boats to race around the world the wrong way (east to west). In summary, it is optimised for sailing upwind in 30 - 50 kts, and extremely seaworthy."

As the temperatures fell and the weather challenged *2041* and her crew, there was a salutary reminder of the power of the ocean. The wind was blowing up to 40 knots while first mate Emily was winching on the furling line. She takes up the story of what happened next: "A huge wave came washing down the side deck. There was a lot of force in the water and before I knew it, I was washed down the deck and I felt that I was going to be washed off the back of the boat. I was certainly glad that I was clipped on and also that I was able to hold onto the winch handle that I was using at the time.

"The other problem was that my lifejacket inflated which winded me and then meant I got pinned down onto the deck....In the end I hauled myself out and got below so I could get my lifejacket off. I was fine

As temperatures began to fall the crew dressed accordingly - pictured above Gorden Clute, P&O Nedlloyd, USA, who was one of the most experienced sailors to join the crew.

Pictured left skipper Mark and first mate Emily studying the charts as they approach the notorious Le Maire Channel.

but a bit shocked."

The beauty of the ocean and sky, the experience of sailing, has been described but the sound of sailing in *2041* has not. Jamie's graphic description brings the sound to life: "I'm convinced that the boat's alive; she groans and creaks continuously. Lying in my bunk the mast is just to my right and all the noises from the rigging and sails is transferred into the hull via the mast.

"On my left the water rushes and pounds against the hull only inches from my head. The duty watch has just taken to the foredeck to change the sails;

Challenging seas met 2041's crew as she headed south into the Roaring Forties. Pictured above Matty Hakvoort from One Thousand Steps, the Netherlands.

directly overhead boots stamp, winches grind, the sails and boom flap in the wind. To add to this cacophony the propeller, which is locked from turning, sings like a tuning fork. The faster the boat moves the higher the pitch. There is no explanation for the propeller singing, some just do it. When the weather is rough all of these sounds bring a freight train to mind.

"Now consider the motion of the boat. First of all it never stops. If the seas are head-on she pitches; if the seas are from the beam she rolls. Usually the seas are confused and so is the boat so she rolls and pitches. The heavier the sea the more violent the motion making everyday tasks extremely difficult. Any loose objects fly about and most of the secured things rattle and shake. The combination of the noise and motion from the "working" of the boat remind me of Jonah and the whale."

Five days after leaving Mar del Plata *2041* had reached the same latitude south as England is north and the skipper recorded in his diary: "We have a real reason to be proud of what we have achieved. Yesterday was a record breaking day. Not only did we beat the top speed for the trip so far but we also broke the 200nm in a day for the first time with 202nm from noon to noon. We are right in the thick of it now with the lows sweeping across our path."

In their report of the voyage, Matty and Paul identified clearly the aims of taking part in a *2041* voyage - firstly to raise awareness of Antarctica and the environment, secondly to sail in some of the most desolate and beautiful places and thirdly to experience a thrilling adventure.

They explained how each member of the crew decided to make a plan of action following the voyage, including the idea of presenting a story to inspire children. They quoted Antoine de Saint-Exupery who said: "If you want to build a ship, don't start to gather instruments and wood, but first teach shipbuilders to long for the sea."

Paul and Matty recognised in themselves the same romantic idealism which inspired Swan to follow in the footsteps of Scott and subsequently to set up Mission Antarctica. They said: "Robert Swan is partly a romantic hero to us, searching for a lost paradise, but we are sure the effect of this ideal will have a realistic and positive influence on the future of Antarctica."

Though the skipper and crew had been concerned about the Le Maire Strait it proved relatively straightforward and *2041* was escorted through to safety by a pod of whales before the yacht turned into the Beagle Channel.

Mark said: "I was quite moved by a quiet glance south and realising that at that moment there was nothing but 600 miles of sea separating us from Antarctica itself. After a long journey I at that moment realised 'we had made it.'"

Saskia described the sight that met their eyes: "After seven days without seeing land, this is the most beautiful land we ever saw: rough rocks partly covered with snow at Staten Island, and green hills along with more rocks at Tierra del Fuego. This place has always been an exotic spot on the chart, a place for pirates and adventurers. And now we ourselves are sailing along the beautiful landscape of the Strait of Le Maire!

"At lunch time we saw whales! We had almost given up hope of seeing any, but in the last piece of deep water that we will be sailing during this leg,

2041 in Ushuaia.

three whales appeared a few hundred metres away. We saw their fins and backs breaking the water."

The crew who sailed *2041* to Ushuaia broke some of the yacht's own records. They told strange jokes, sang sailing songs and enjoyed flute concerts from Emily and, above all, they got *2041* to Ushuaia in time to meet the challenge of Antarctica.

Antarctica

The team who gathered in Ushuaia at the very tip of South America ready to take part in *2041's* historic voyage to Antarctica included Nicolas Bayle from Vopak, France; Nicole Picot from Wijsmuller, Argentina; Grant Barnard from P&O Nedlloyd, South Africa; Bob Macauley from Miles of Smiles, USA and Annie McEwen-Holder from One Step Beyond Expeditions, UK. They were joined by four further crew members from the Netherlands - Yvonne van der Velde, from Rabobank, Paul Mulder and Herman Rijnders from Heerema and Ton van den Berg from Philips.

On 7 March the yacht left Ushuaia heading for Puerto Williams where the crew were to spend their last night before heading out into the Drake Passage.

Skipper Mark wrote: "Arriving in Puerto Williams in the dark created an interesting pilotage exercise. The Yacht Club is hidden up a small muddy creak which is completely unlit. We came in with just 40cm under the keel with fishing boats strewn up on the banks well above the tide line. It was a really a special moment for me, stepping off the yacht onto the sunken ship they use as a yacht club because, in 1992 I passed through Puerto Williams on a kayak and left a paddle here. Finding it still on display with all the expedition sig-

> **Captain's Log:**
> Ushuaia - Ushuaia
> Depart - 6/3//00
> Arrive - 23/3/00
> Distance - 1461nm
> Estimated time - 19 days
> Actual time - 17 days

Pictured above, left to right, Bob Macauley from Miles of Smiles, USA; Annie Holder from One Step Beyond Expeditions, UK and Grant Barnard from P&O Nedlloyd.

Pictured above, left to right, Herman Rijnders from Heerema in the Netherlands; 2041 engineer Neil Shuttleworth and Nicolas Bayle from Vopak, France.

natures still on it brought the memories flooding back."

The next day *2041* nosed out of Puerto Williams to face the major challenge of her voyage south - the Drake Passage.   As Paul explained: "For people who have never heard of the Drake Passage, it is to sailors as Mount Everest is to a mountaineer. It's one of the roughest seas in the world."

Annie, who had worked for Robert Swan for the last five years, little thought that her research work would one day find her on a yacht bound for Antarctica. She wrote: "We all had our fears about the Drake Passage but we are wondering if we have taken the wrong course, we have flat seas and the sun shone brightly today - all we need to wear is shorts and T-shirts! However, we are always aware of the old adage 'the calm before the storm'.

"They are a good bunch of people who are very committed to making change a reality. The watch teams are now back in business, having had dinner and a special treat from Nicolas, from Vopak, who brought us all a 'goodie bag' full of various sweets from his home town in France. He is a real diamond who has been as steady as a rock throughout our bout of seasickness."

Nicole echoed these sentiments when she wrote: "During this trip friendships were formed, joining different people of different countries, and we all know that these friendships will continue after our return. We will remember the laughs, the seasickness, the worries and the delight of sharing such an extraordinary expedition, although we may be apart, we shall always remember this team and our friends."

Pictured above Nicole Picot from Wijsmuller, Argentina and below, Paul Mulder from Heerema, the Netherlands.

A few days out from land, the skipper discovered that the stern gland for the prop shaft appeared to be leaking. The concern was that if the seal suddenly went the yacht could potentially take on lots of water in an area where they would be far from help. The skipper faced a difficult decision but finally, having weighed all the pros and cons, decided to carry on heading south.

Once past the Antarctic convergence zone the crew had to keep a continuous watch for ice. The skipper wrote: "The temperature is really dropping off now. We have a sea temperature of four degrees and falling fast. Today we are starting formal ice watches which add another element to the situation. Ice watches are a game of hide and seek. During the day, we have the advantage while at night the ice takes the upper hand.... The ice that we really have to watch out for are small chunks of ice about the size of a car. These are called Growlers.

"There is for some reason, a real sensation of desolation and isolation. The sea fog came in last night for the first time. I hate fog. Normally I hate it because you cannot see the rocks and other boats but there are none of those down here. I fear the ice. We have now closed the front watertight bulkhead as a precaution. On deck the temperatures are dropping to near freezing during the hours of darkness which means the crew pile on the layers of clothes every time they are shaken from their bunks to relieve the on-watch team."

Entering Antarctic waters also meant the crew had to carefully follow the protocols of the Antarctic Treaty with regard to any waste produced by the yacht or the crew. Yvonne explained: "A point of interest in Antarctica is what to do with waste. It is absolutely forbidden to leave any kind of waste behind. This means that we do the dishes with water and some lemon juice, and that all the waste is collected in separate bags and buckets."

Finally on 11 March they saw land - snow capped mountains. Bob was moved by what he saw: "Ever since King George Island came into sight yesterday morning, I've been overcome by this land's utter uniqueness. Every other place I've ever been could be understood by analogy - like the mountains back home but bigger, like the cathedral I once saw only grander... Even the places that pushed the limits of analogy fit into a pre-existing image - "That's how I pictured the Himalayas," and so on.

"But analogy and preconception are of no assistance here, for each glance at this land reminds me that this is like no place I've ever been, or even imagined. Not mere snowy hills like the winter coast-lines of home, nor icebergs akin to those in films like "Titanic". The ice envelops the land, as if a mammoth wave from aeons ago was frozen in mid-rush, a hulking presence that comes as close to the proverbial 'immovable object' as can be imagined. It's no wonder that scientists here call water 'liquid ice'."

When they arrived at Bellingshausen, late in the afternoon, they had finally made it. It was an amazing moment for all concerned. *2041's* skipper Mark summed it up when he wrote: "We left England on the 27 December 1999 and have travelled almost 9,000nm to get here. We have encountered mechanical difficulties, gales, maddening calms, some wonderful sailing and have visited some fantastic places.

"Some experts said that we would not make it to Bellingshausen; others even put these thoughts in print. These guys did not know what a Challenge yacht can do and did not expect the resilience of the team that has got her here. Yes it has taken a mam-

2041's crew prove all their critics wrong and arrive at Bellingshausen to help with the clean up operation. They are pictured here taking a lunch break.

moth effort from a great many people and without this effort I am sure we would not have made it this far."

Nicolas wrote, on the same day: "This first day in Antarctica, sailing along King George Island was a marvellous day: the panorama looks like the Himalayas but with sea, penguins, seal and whales in foreground.

"The day was magic and suddenly, we altered course to port and entered a small bay and discovered Bellingshausen, the first goal of the mission: the panorama is completely different, austere buildings and mountains of wastes, drums and plastics.

"Nevertheless, if this station is not the most beau-

A gentoo penguin takes a closer look at 2041's dinghy!

tiful view of Antarctica, the Russians are the most brave guys in all this area: living at this base for 18 months at a time, far from their family and friends, and working every day in hard conditions is impressive, very impressive.

"If you walk away from the rusty oil tanks structures just a few hundred metres, you are in the rough wilderness again, as we imagine Antarctica when the first explorers came, and it is beautiful, so beautiful."

At Bellingshausen the yacht was surrounded by gentoo penguins, curious to have a good look at 2041 and her crew. One penguin decided to jump on board the dinghy for a closer inspection!

2041 spent a few days at Bellingshausen, giving the crew time to visit various parts of the island. Herman went to the nearby Chilean base and wrote: "This base is a different world compared to the Russian base. It's more like a small village with a post office, souvenir shop, even a small school for those who bring their families.

"We had a very hearty welcome from the base commander who gave us a guided tour around the base. We visited the school, Paul had the flag from his daughter's school in Zierikzee signed by all the kids and teachers of the school, photographs were taken with all the teddys we brought and e-mail addresses were exchanged. This may well be the beginning of a long lasting relationship between schools in the Netherlands and the Southernmost school in the world."

The crew took extra provisions and presents for the Russians, spent time talking to them and surveyed the shoreline to check sea levels for the large ship which will need to enter the bay to remove rubbish from Bellingshausen.

The team had set out as total strangers but, by the time they reached the Antarctic they had developed a strong team spirit as Grant explained: "I would never have thought that I would be in Antarctica running from the warmth and comfort (three degrees Celsius last night) of the Dog House to the foredeck to check the anchor mooring in stitches of laughter whilst getting tangled up in my safety harness as a wave rises and crashes over me soaking the last of my semi-dry clothes.

"It is not the making light of a difficult or trying situation, but rather staying positive and coping with life at sea, dealing with whatever conditions are presented. The weather dictates and you determine the outcome of your day.

"When working the yacht your hands are wet first and you feel cold, then nothing. When you run into

Pictured above Ton van den Berg from Philips, the Netherlands and below, Yvonne van der Velde from Rabobank, also in the Netherlands.

the engine room to warm them up they start to burn like walking on hot tar barefoot. A hot cup of coffee has never tasted this good.

"After starting out as complete strangers the twelve crew members of *2041* have bonded by sharing experiences, difficult situations exercising patience not to mention a few hundred laughs a day. The result being a crew that rises to the occasion under the competent leadership and guidance of Mark, Emily and Neil."

Near Bellingshausen the crew sailed close to the remains of an old whaling station. Paul wrote: "It is creepy to think that in the heyday of this industry, they killed over 5,000 whales each season. The remains of these animals can be found all over the place and, if you think those were the old days you are wrong. As we all know, there are still countries who believe it is necessary to slaughter these beautiful animals for luxury goods or so called science."

On 14 March the yacht headed away from Bellingshausen for Deception Island and arrived in the shelter of the volcanic island just in time before a terrifying Antarctic blizzard closed in.

During the night they had a 75 knot gust, equivalent to gale force 12. The storm did not abate the next day and the crew were frightened. Finally at lunchtime the anchor pulled away from its hold and, in the teeth of the gale they had to winch it up and try to secure it again.

Emily wrote: "It was almost impossible to see without ski goggles and trying to breathe while facing into the wind wasn't easy either. All the snow and ice we'd seen on top of the mountain the day before was now at the bottom and we could see pieces of ice being blown past us. The boat was covered in a layer of ice and a light dusting of snow; it was like a skating rink."

Nicolas was one of the few sponsor crew members with sailing experience and he described the frightening scene of being adrift in an Antarctic storm: "The wind during our period at Deception Island was incredible: more than 74 knots, 130km/h !!! The anchor watch was not a pleasure, especially when you have to go forward in this wind carrying ice to check if all was OK with the anchor and the additional safety hooks.

engine on to help hold the yacht in place and prevent the anchor dragging loose again.

The next day the storm finally blew itself out. The crew however had been shaken up by the storm and most now wanted to head for home, without seeing mainland Antarctica. For a time the atmosphere on the yacht was strained but, as the weather cleared and with a good forecast, the crew decided they would head

Above the force 12 storm which swept over Deception Island bringing some worrying moments for 2041's crew and right, a beautiful calm followed the storm.

"And suddenly we were adrift. Herman and I were immediately on the deck to heave up the anchor, to prepare for the next anchorage. Mark was busy with the wheel so, as I was the only professional sailor on board used to take navigation and safety decisions, Mark told me to find the best anchor position. To reach a good position with a 60 knots wind on a 20 metre vessel in this bad visibility was not easy, but we made it. Thanks to Herman, Mark and I, the vessel and the crew are alive (I am serious!) This experience was terrific for some of us but for others it was terrifying."

Finally the anchor held fast again though, because of the strength of the storm, they had to keep the further south where they saw breathtaking scenery at Trinity Island. This was the furthest point south - 65 degrees.

March is late in the Antarctic season and the ice was already thick. The skipper was concerned that the yacht could get trapped so they did not stay long before heading north into safer waters. The voyage back across the Drake Passage was uneventful with the region's notorious weather nowhere to be seen.

Ton wrote in his diary: "We are sailing to Cape Horn over the Drake passage, while Cape petrels and albatrosses accompany *2041* towards the convergence zone.

"We are heading home through again a calm Drake without wind. Ready to show everyone the photographs we took and the adventures we have been through. We saw something of the beauty of Antarctic and the pollution on King George Island and once more we realise how important it is to save this unspoiled wilderness."

Bob wrote: "One evening Emily played her flute for us, and as if in response to the sounds of "Carmen" coming from the middle of the Southern Ocean, a school of dolphins raced with us, playing at our bow, lingering long past sunset, the only time we'd seen dolphin the entire trip. And this morning, as the infamous Cape Horn came into view, the very place where Captain Bligh and the *Bounty* finally turned back after trying for four weeks to round it, there was Neil up on the foredeck, whistling away, as if daring Neptune to show us "the real Cape Horn," even as we motored north on flat seas.

"Our journey is nearly finished, and the piercing beauty that I'd anticipated three weeks ago is now a cherished memory. And though our time there was

Mission accomplished - Emily and Mark pictured at Cape Horn after 2041's successful voyage to Antarctica.

brief, I believe we were all changed by Antarctica in some way; I know I have been."

On returning to Ushuaia the crew were met by Swan who shared with them a mixture of elation at their marvellous achievement and relief that they were once more safe on dry land. Herman spoke for all when he wrote: "We left Ushuaia sixteen days ago, not knowing what to expect, what we would encounter, whether we could cope with it, everybody with his own personal feelings and expectations. Now it's time to make up the balance and everybody will do that in their own way."

The Russians

The arrival of *2041* in Antarctica was a tangible achievement, a moment for all concerned to stand still for a moment and indulge in a feeling of pride.   In that moment of stopping to think, those involved realised that *2041's* voyage had become an end in itself.   The experience was so intense, even for those watching from Europe, that *2041's* place in the bigger picture had gone slightly out of focus.

Now, as *2041* and her crew rested in South America, the picture snapped clearly back to sharp reality. *2041* is only a small part of the story which began all those years ago when Swan dreamed of following in the footsteps of Scott.

The chain of events this set in motion led in 1994 to the One Step Beyond Expedition to Antarctica of 35 young people from nations around the world. This expedition achieved its aims of peace and the promotion of international understanding but left one question - how to build on the experiences of the young people in the future so that the aims of their expedition would never be forgotten?

The answer was clear - the young explorers had visited the Russian scientific research station at Bellingshausen and seen with their own eyes the difficulties of balancing economic and environmental needs.   To continue the work of the One Step Beyond Expedition by helping the Russians clear rubbish from Bellingshausen was a perfect solution. This would involve continued international co-operation and would have the practical aim of clearing 1,000 tons of rubbish from Antarctica.   This was how Mission Antarctica was born.

Because of his close friendship with Dr. Misha Malakhov, Swan knew all too well the harsh economic conditions facing people in post-Communist Russia.   This was a country struggling to pro-

Pictured this page a penguin wanders across the Bellingshausen site and, opposite, Russian engineers at work transferring liquid waste from rusting metal containers to sturdy new plastic barrels.

vide for its people, there was no extra cash lying around to pay for the expensive operation of taking waste materials away from a research station at the other end of the globe.

In the height of the Cold War, Bellingshausen Research Station in Maxwell Bay on the south eastern end of King George Island, was manned by scores of scientists. They were carrying out some of the most important research in Antarctica however, in the past two decades this work has been curtailed. This meant that buildings and machinery became redundant and was left to rust and rot.

If resources had been ploughed into moving the rubbish then the scientific work would have undoubtedly suffered. By holding out the hand of international friendship the research work could be saved and today at Bellingshausen scientists contin-ue to work on meteorological measurements, satellite remote sensing observations, upper atmosphere research and biological studies.

The Russians are proud and capable people, probably the most capable of any nation at coping with the rigours of extreme conditions. Their experience of the Arctic is second to none but, as the tragedy of the *Kursk* so graphically illustrated, all the experience in the world cannot compensate for a lack of resources.

Mission Antarctica was a project almost without parallel. It was a private operation, inspired by the ideas of young people, to do something practical to save the Antarctica wilderness. Over the next five years experts from Europe visited Bellingshausen to quantify the waste to be removed and to work out the logistics.

It is easy to forget that Bellingshausen lies 600 miles from civilisation, across some of the most dangerous seas in the world. The base has no quay side, just a stony beach and, for nine months of the year it is completely inaccessible, locked in by ice.

Following earlier initial surveys, in 1999 a full report was made by waste management experts appointed by Mission Antarctica. The urgent conclusions point-

ed to problems like liquid waste being stored in rusting metal barrels - the following year plastic barrels were taken to Bellingshausen so the liquids could be transferred and would no longer leak.

The Bellingshausen report accurately measured and identified all the rubbish so that plans could be laid to take a large ship into the base to remove at least 1000 tons of scrap metal and other rubbish. The report identified those buildings and facilities which were in good condition, equipment which was no longer required and could be sold as well as all the material which could be recycled.

Pictured above Mission Antarctica's team 2000 working on filling sacks to remove an enormous pile of salt.

Right - the Russian engineers' team leader Valerie from Ryazan.

A further problem identified by the report, apart from the weather conditions at Bellingshausen, was the fact that the scrap materials were spread over a large area of difficult terrain. Before a ship could be chartered to remove the rubbish, it would all have to be collected on the shore. This was a massive task and, over the next few Antarctic seasons, Mission Antarctica paid for Russian engineers to undertake this work.

Bronco Lane, has taken a close personal interest in the work at Bellingshausen and led the team who surveyed the rubbish. He explains how he met Swan and became involved in Mission Antarctica: "I first met Robert in 1993 when he had been assisting his friend and Russian Polar hero, Misha Malakhov to establish "Centre Pole" the first commercial polar guiding outfit in Russia.

"Some time later I received a call from Robert asking me if I was interested in selecting, training and looking after a group of 35 young people, from 25 nations some of whom were in conflict, on a visit to Antarctica, aboard a Russian ship. My only query was to ask rather timidly if the ship had sails or an engine, as yachtsman I am not! This was to be my first visit to the southern continent and I became fascinated by its unique status for international science and the fragile environmental treaty which defends it from man's avaricious exploitation. The young people's reaction was inspirational and from it grew Robert's concept of helping the Russians honour their commitment to the treaty, by removing their waste from Bellingshausen for recycling."

Russian engineers working to remove a dis-used and dangerous asbestos pipe from King George's Island, Antarctica.

Bronco's personal involvement continued when he travelled to Bellingshausen with the waste management experts: "In 1999 I took a team of waste and environmental management representatives to inspect and record the size of the problem. On arrival we were met on the beach at 3am by the booming and cheerful voice of Colonel Constantin, base commander and the St. Petersburg equivalent of Rowan Atkinson. 'Bronco', he would explain, 'we do not have very much here, except our sense of humour. As a former military person you will know how vital that is to good morale!' So, with bouts of hilarious mime and lots of bear hugs, we would spend a week recording and categorising everything to be removed.

"Working alongside the first two Russian engineers from Ryazan, selected by Misha, we gathered the vital logistical information necessary for outloading the rubbish by sea. More than anything else, I was learning how proud and human our Russian colleagues were, as they refused to become despondent when hearing of the daily slide of the rouble (and their wages) some 10,000 miles away.

"Having spent most of my life as a Special Forces operational soldier and mountaineer, I am acutely conscious of how critical to an isolated team's high

morale is the provision of nutritional and attractive food. Nothing illustrated to me more the situation Russia finds itself in than the Bellingshausen Base food situation. The staff survive on a boring diet of basic dried foodstuffs, with very little supplement of fresh vegetables, fruit or eggs. There was a keen off duty interest in fishing being driven by a need to add extra nutrition. Add to this situation a cook closely resembling Rab C. Nesbitt, who completely ignored aspects of customer service and was forced to stick religiously to a daily menu dictated from Russia, and you understand the problem."

The engineers worked hard to sort and gather the rubbish during the Antarctic summer and their efforts were impressive. When Bronco returned to Bellingshausen in early 2000 he wrote:

"I was delighted to see how the situation had

Pictured above engineers working to cut up scrap metal into moveable lengths.

Right - engineers working to move the asbestos pipes to a safe storage point.

improved, following a full season's clean up by eight Russian engineers sponsored by Mission Antarctica. Ably led by Valerie, they had successfully transformed the whole aspect of the base, raising everyone's morale and self respect. A dynamic sports man and Arctic guide, Valerie had sufficient energy left to swim daily in an ice fed lake and run a weekly marathon around King George Island.

"Valerie is returning again for the 2001 season with another team to compact the 1000 tons of scrap metals in readiness for extraction by sea in January 2002. I am hoping the cook has been replaced before I return too, in January 2001!"

Bronco's motto, from an ancient Chinese philosopher is: "Better to light a candle - than complain of the dark!" It seems very clear that the work at Bellingshausen by Mission Antarctica teams closely follows this philosophy.

Soon after Bronco's visit, *2041* nosed her way into Maxwell Bay giving the crew first hand experience of the work of Mission Antarctica. The Russians soon had some willing volunteers from *2041's* crew, who worked at putting a huge pile of salt into bags as well as surveying the bay to check depths and logistics for the ship which will remove the rubbish between January and March 2002.

Before *2041* left King George's Island, the new

Bellingshausen Russian research station with 2041 moored nearby in Maxwell Bay.

Bellingshausen commander, Oleg, visited the yacht for a farewell celebration.

Skipper Mark wrote: "Our visit has been a fantastic insight into life at an Antarctic research station. From what I have seen of the base the Russians have been working very hard gathering the rubbish into manageable piles ready for the removal operation. The plans that the Bellingshausen team talk about show real determination makes a difference. It is great to be able to assist them in their task through Mission Antarctica."

Swan raised the funds for Mission Antarctica from sponsor companies keen to be involved in making a statement of commitment to the environment. The one problem with a project such as this was it is hard

Rubbish piled on the shore of Maxwell Bay ready for collection.

success. The resources we have are limited and it's true to say that without the support of Mission Antarctica and all our generous sponsors, the rubbish would not be removed from the Russian station at Bellingshausen.

"I look forward to the final removal of the rubbish in early 2002 and I would like to send many, many thanks to all who have helped."

There is still one enormous task to undertake - the actual removal of the rubbish. For this Mission Antarctica needs to raise funds to charter a ship capable of the task.

to out-reach a story about rubbish. It is far too down to earth and practical to make exciting reading, however worthwhile the project is. The yacht *2041* was the ideal way of adding an element of adventure and a means of out-reaching the story to the world. Even better, she could actually take people to see for themselves the work that was being carried out at Bellingshausen.

So, *2041's* place in the story of Bellingshausen is firmly booked. She might be a racehorse of the seas, but her beauty is being used to attract attention to the strength of the cart horse task of clearing rubbish from the world's last great wilderness.

Dr. Misha Malakhov, hero of Russia, said: "The joint co-operation between Mission Antarctica and the Russian Antarctic Expedition has been a great

The Voyage Continues

In December 2000 the first of three voyages to Antarctica will begin. Following on from the success of primary school headteacher Chris Bulloch's participation in Mission Antarctica, the first voyage of *2041* will include those who work with young people. The participants will be ten teachers from eight different nations, and the voyage is intended to inspire and motivate them in their work.

Swan said: "It's crucially important that teachers, who are often not respected or appreciated for the work they do, are given this once in a lifetime opportunity which they can then use in their future work. Each individual has

2041 will make three further journeys to Antarctica before March 2001.

been challenged to find ways of making the Mission Antarctica story meaningful in their schools and communities."

The second voyage which will begin in January will be made up of an international group of ten Royal & SunAlliance employees from eight nations. They will be closely involved with the progress of the teachers' voyage as their challenge is to get the message out through technology to young people. In other words, how can young people be encouraged and motivated by the Mission Antarctica story and the website? The voyage is already full and the selection process is under way.

The third voyage will be made up of a number of other corporate sponsors, including Merrill Lynch, Knight Frank, BUPA and Lever Bros. The theme of this voyage will be to get the message out to business people on a global basis as well as to young people.

Mark Hopking will continue as *2041's* skipper with Emily Pearson as first mate. They will be joined by a new engineer, 41-year-old Mike Tattersfield who is a Yorkshireman by birth. Mike served in the Royal Navy where he qualified as Chief Petty Officer Marine Engineering. He spent twelve years working as an artificer and has served

*2041's new engineer
Mike Tattersfield
and below
Siaron Glanridd-Jones
from Royal &
SunAlliance*

on *HMS Endurance*.

During the same period Bronco Lane will be leading a separate expedition to Bellingshausen on a recce of the large storage tanks. His expedition will be made up of people from Standard Life, Forum Invest, the International Award and long term supporters. He will also be finalising, with technical support from Wijsmuller, the details of the removal of the rubbish in 2002. At the same time Mission Antarctica has employed Russian engineers to continue the clean up.

Bronco will also take part in a visit to Buenos Aires, along with Adrian Evans and a representative from Wijsmuller. This meeting is scheduled to take place in early February 2001 and will involve discussions with Argentinian waste experts on the safe disposal of the rubbish from Bellingshausen.

Mission Antarctica managing director Adrian Evans said: "It is critical that we can show results to all sponsors past, present and future. Therefore we have agreed a timetable and will remove the rubbish from Bellingshausen in January 2002. As much as possible of the waste will be recycled in Buenos Aires."

There has been excellent support from sponsors all round, and particularly from Royal & SunAlliance. Mr. Bob Mendelsohn, Group Chief Executive, Royal & SunAlliance Insurance Group Plc said: "As a prominent worldwide organisation we take our own environmental policies seriously as part of a broad commitment to responsible corporate citizenship.

"Our support for Mission Antarctica and the preservation of the last great wilderness on earth is a practical and positive example of our commitment to act as responsible custodians of our world. But what has this to do with a global financial services company?

"As one of the world's largest insurers of businesses, we incur claims and losses when our clients damage the environment. We have the ability to make a positive impact by advising our clients how to minimise environmental impact, and protect their own communities.

"By improving the efficiency of our internal processes, particularly energy use and waste management; we can also reduce the potential for negative environmental impact from our own activities.

"The most important reason is because its simply the right thing to do. We aim to be a "dominant force" in our industry and that means being the leader; setting the agenda in all aspects of what we do throughout the world.

"2041 is a great "flagship" for the mission, and we at Royal & SunAlliance are privileged to have helped support its launch. Aptly named, it provides an extremely powerful reminder of the significance of the Antarctic Treaty and our collective responsibility to inspire young people throughout the world to protect this special place for future generations.

"We wish the crew, supporters and all participants in the forthcoming expeditions our continued support, and every success in the challenges that lie ahead."

The following thoughts from Siaron Glanrid-Jones from Royal & SunAlliance who took part in the expedition 2000 to Bellingshausen, sum up the feelings of those who take part in Mission Antarctica.

Siaron said: "The prospect of spending every living, breathing moment for a whole month with eight people you've never met before was an interesting challenge. By the time we parted we weren't eight strangers. We were a team.

"Being part of the Mission is something that makes me really proud to work for Royal & SunAlliance.   What the Expedition team 2000 did was very special.   Anyone with enough money can pay to go down to the Antarctic - what everyone doesn't get the opportunity to do is stay on a scientific base like Bellingshausen for nearly two weeks, living and working with the Russian team there.

"You can prepare yourself for the scenery and the wildlife. Anyone   who's   fortunate enough to visit the Antarctic will know before they go that it's going to be stunning. What took me by surprise was some of the fascinating people we were privileged to meet along the way, not least of which the Russians at the scientific base on King George Island where we stayed".

As to the future, once 2041 has made her final three voyages to Antarctica, she will then turn towards   warmer   climates, embarking on a world tour to publicise the work of Mission Antarctica.

Her first port of call, in April

Pictured above Mr. Bob Mendelsohn, Group Chief Executive, Royal & SunAlliance Group Plc.

2001, will be South Africa where she will be over-hauled following her two years work in Antarctica. Following the re-fit in South Africa, 2041 will embark on her three year round the world tour which will end with the yacht finally returning to the place where the dreams began - in the Netherlands.

The voyage of 2041 will take her thousands of miles around the globe. The adventures along the way will no doubt be amazing

2041 in Antarctica - her mission to preserve this continent, the world's last great wilderness

ness, Swan kept his vision clear. His message and his achievements reach the hearts of people across all social classes, across all continents and will span the test of time.

Swan has brought his very special combination of skills to lead, to think, to speak and to inspire others. His message touches business people, inspires school children, shocks drug addicts and shames political leaders.

Swan said: "It's been a long process from asking our 'customers', the young people, what we should do to inspire, through the reconnaissance stages, the employment of the fantastic Russian engineers in accordance with our joint co-operation to the purchase of *2041* and her maiden voyage.

"We are now closing in on the result that's necessary - the removal of 1000 tons of rubbish from Bellingshausen station in 2002 and of course the communication to young people in 44 nations about the preservation of the Antarctic.

"I am so proud of the performance of the crew and the team who have made this possible. I would like to personally thank them all and, above all, thank our extremely generous sponsors."

A lesser person would have given up years ago. Instead Swan continues to work for Antarctica first and foremost. A yacht voyage is not much, but it can inspire people to action. A thousand tons of rubbish is not much, but it will make a lasting difference. A few words are not much, but they can change the world.

tales in themselves. To every place *2041* visits she will bring a little magic, not just from the wide oceans, but from the ice at the end of the Earth.

The aim of the round the world voyage is to get at least 20 million young people to commit to preserving Antarctica. Swan believes that every government will listen to the voices of so many, especially when the mission will have another 38 years to attract votes.

Swan's voyage through life has been something of a pilgrimage - from the boy inspired by heroic tales to the man facing the knowledge of his seeming powerlessness in the face of the environmental destruction of Antarctica, the place he loves so much.

Undeterred by being only one voice in a wilder-

The Yacht 2041

Principal Technical Specifications

Length Overall: 67'
Draft: 3.15m
Beam: 5.25m
Mast height: 85'
Weight of keel: 12 tonnes
Hull: Mild Steel
Deck: Stainless Steel
Number of berths: 13
Cruising speed: 7.5 knots/180nm per 24 hour period

Fuel: 2,500ltrs
Water capacity: 1000ltrs
Main Engine: Perkins Sabre 180 turbo charged
De-sailination (sea water to Fresh water): 2 ltrs/min
Sails made by Hoods Sailmakers, UK
Sail Area: 247m squared
Waterline Length: 55'
Displ. (full load): 43.4 tonnes
Constructed: Plymouth, England - Devonport Royal Navy Dockyard

This shot of 2041 from the mast was taken by Nicolas Bayle in Antarctica.

Voyage Maps

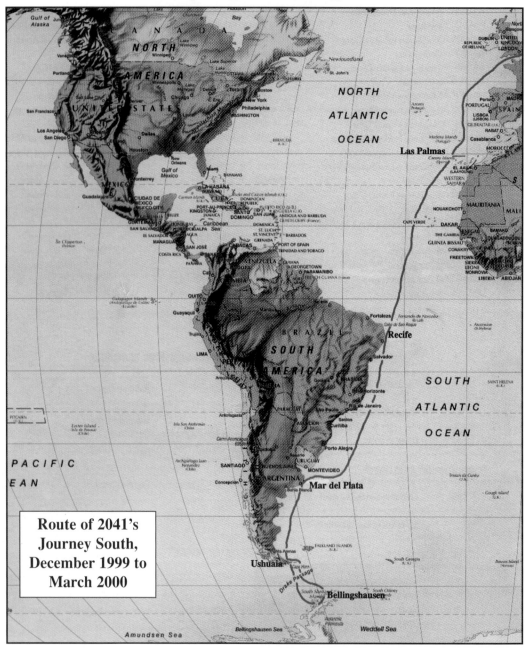

Route of 2041's
Journey South,
December 1999 to
March 2000

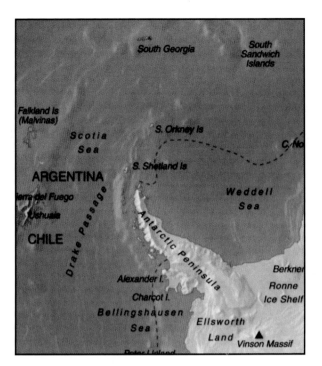

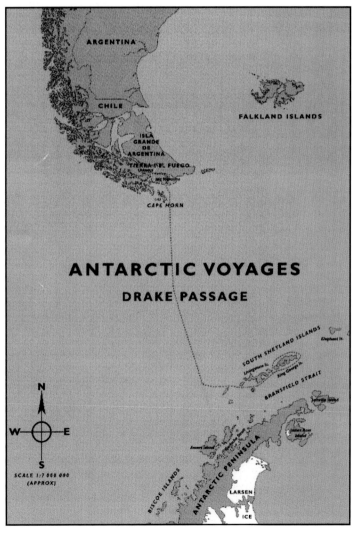

Route of 2041's
Antarctic Voyage
Feb-March 2000

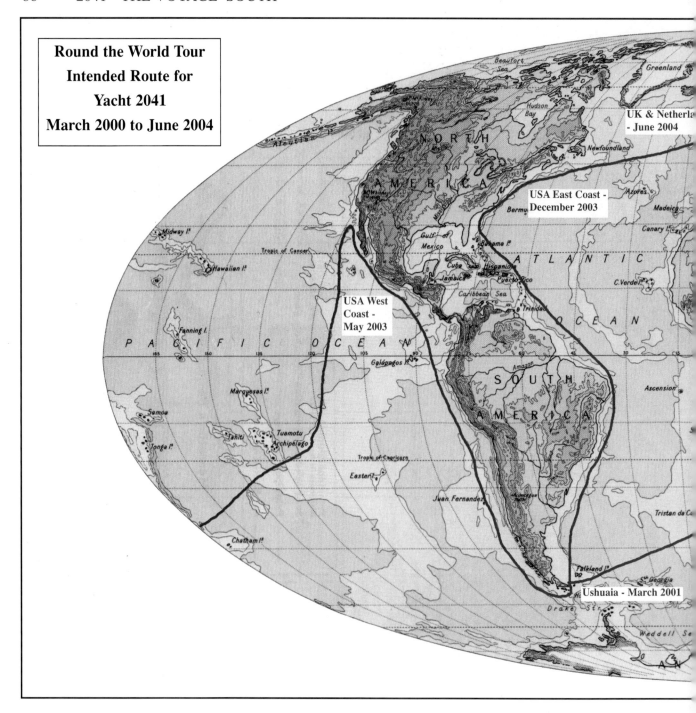

Round the World Tour
Intended Route for
Yacht 2041
March 2000 to June 2004

UK & Netherla
- June 2004

USA East Coast -
December 2003

USA West
Coast -
May 2003

Ushuaia - March 2001

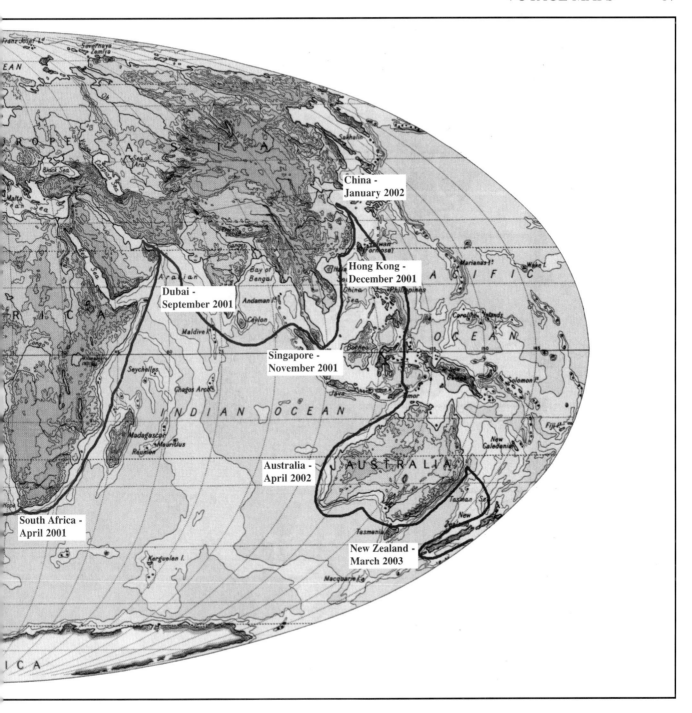

China -
January 2002

Hong Kong -
December 2001

Dubai -
September 2001

Singapore -
November 2001

Australia -
April 2002

South Africa -
April 2001

New Zealand -
March 2003

Mission Antarctica would like to thank the following companies for their support:

Bever; Bouwfonds Nederlandse; Citizen Watches; Damen Shipyards Group;
Datema Rotterdam; Dubarry; Electronic Devices Ltd.; Forum Invest;
Geveke Motoren BV; Gill Ocean Gear; Halyard Insulation;
Heijmans; Honda Marine Group; Hood Sailmakers;
KLM Royal Dutch Airlines; KPMG; L. J. Harri BV;
Mees Pierson Private Bank & Trust; Meissner Winches;
Meursing & Partners Corporate Communications;
Northern Diver Europe; Perkins Engines; Port of Rotterdam;
Radio Holland Marine; Royal Maas Yacht Club;
Sailtron BV; Schiphol Group;
Schweitzer, Blaisse, Rinnooy Kan & Co. Perception Management;
Staalkabel BV; Station 12; Rotterdam City Development Corporation;
The Veerhaven Foundation; US Paint Division Europe; Van den Akker; Zodiac.

THE CREW

Permanent Crew 1999-2000: Mark Hopking (captain), Emily Pearson (first mate), Neil Shuttleworth (engineer)

Permanent Crew 2000-2001: Mark Hopking (captain), Emily Pearson (first mate), Mike Tattersfield (engineer)

ADDITIONAL CREW MEMBERS:

The Netherlands - UK: Meg Jim, P&O Nedlloyd, Hong Kong.

Lymington - Plymouth:
Jonathan Lewis, P&O Nedlloyd, New Zealand;   Anne-Marie Janssen, Rabobank, Netherlands;
Wouter Bak, Philips, Netherlands;   Teo Seow Ling, Vopak, Singapore;
Frans Hogenhout, Wijsmuller, Netherlands.

Plymouth - Las Palmas:
Marty van de Ven, Philips, Netherlands;   Veronique Duivelshof, Philips, Netherlands;
Paul Lugard, Philips, Netherlands;   Chris Spencer, UK and Ian Taylor, UK.

Las Palmas - Recife:
Eric Strautins, Vopak, Australia;   Veronique Duivelshof, Philips, Netherlands;
Hans P. J. Stigter, Vopak, Netherlands;   Hans de Willigen, Vopak, Netherlands;
Tom Wain, P&O Nedlloyd, UK.

Recife - Mar del Plata:
Benny Beek, Rabobank, Netherlands;   Frans Hogenhout, Wijsmuller, Netherlands;
Carla Stiekema, Rabobank, Netherlands;   Vincent Peeters, P&O Nedlloyd, Netherlands;
Huub Ehlhardt, Philips, Netherlands;   Leonore Baljon, Vopak, Netherlands;
Robin Ralling, Vopak, Netherlands.

Mar del Plata - Ushuaia:
Gorden Clute, P&O Nedlloyd, USA;   Saskia Blom, Philips, Netherlands;
James Ferguson, Vopak, USA;   Willem Ganzinga, Wijsmuller, Netherlands;
Paul Spaans, One Thousand Steps, Netherlands;   Matty Hakvoort, One Thousand Steps, Netherlands;
Jan Rudolf Westerveld, Rabobank, Netherlands.

Ushuaia - Antarctica:
Nicolas Bayle, Vopak, France;   Yvonne van der Velde, Rabobank, Netherlands;
Grant Barnard, P&O Nedlloyd, South Africa;   Paul Mulder, Heerema, Netherlands;
Nicole Picot, Wijsmuller, Argentina;   Bob Macauley, Miles of Smiles, USA;
Ton van den Berg, Philips, Netherlands;   Herman Rijnders, Heerema, Netherlands;
Annie McEwen-Holder, One Step Beyond Expeditions, UK.

CAPTAIN'S VOYAGE LOG

Leg	Departure Date	Arrival Date	Distance (nautical miles)	Estimated Days	Actual Days	Average Speed
Plymouth - Las Palmas	27/12/99	7/1/00	1537	10	10	6.4kn
Las Palmas - Recife	9/1/00	24/1/00	2606	20	15	7.2kn
Recife - Mar del Plata	29/1/00	12/2/00	2349	16	14	6.9kn
Mar del Plata - Ushuaia	20/2/00	28/2/00	1260	10	8	6.5kn
Ushuaia - Ushuaia	6/3/00	23/3/00	1461	19	17	
Total	27/12/00	23/3/00	9212			6.75kn

MISSION ANTARCTICA PHASES 1-6

Phase 1 - January & February 1997
35 young explorers from 25 different nations visited Antarctica and chose the Russian Bellingshausen Research Station on King George Island as the focus for Mission Antarctica. With the Russian Antarctic Expedition (RAE) the plan to remove waste and renovate the station was made. **Cost of season = £1.2 million**

Phase 2 - January & February 1998
Misha Malakhov and Robert Swan led a survey team and a team from business to Bellingshausen. Morale at the base was at a low ebb. Misha recommended the use of specialist Mission Antarctica team members from Russia. Assisted by Misha, Robert conducted detailed negotiations in Moscow, culminating with the signing of an official Memorandum of Understanding. **Cost of season = £720,000**

Phase 3 - January & February 1999
The work begins with two major undertakings - firstly, the employment of two Russian engineers, sponsored by Mission Antarctica, working alongside the RAE. Secondly, a ten day visit of environmental and waste management experts, led by Bronco Lane, to investigate the nature of the rubbish to be removed and to produce a report. **Cost of season = £550,000**

Phase 4 - 1999/2000
Communication. Mission Antarctica realised that a dynamic means of reaching out to target groups was needed. With the fantastic support of sponsors the yacht *2041* was purchased and refitted. Following a dramatic journey south she visited Bellingshausen Station crewed by sponsor expedition team members. The Russian team continued their rubbish preparation work and a specialist expedition team led by Bronco Lane completed valuable survey work for the final phase in 2002.
Cost of season = £2.1 million (including purchase and refit of yacht)

Phase 5 - January, February & March 2001
Most of the rubbish to be removed is now stacked on the beach but requires serious compacting to make best use of the limited out load resources available. This season, six more Russian engineers, sponsored by Mission Antarctica, will complete the task, plus the removal of 'chemical salt' by filling over 5000 individual sandbags from two former scientific sites. Morale at Bellingshausen is vastly improved, as the RAE can see a tangible result for their co-operation and take pride in a task nearly complete. Mission Antarctica intends to make three voyages by the Yacht *2041* to Antarctica.
Cost of season = £1.3 million

Phase 6 - January, February & March 2002
Between January and March 2002 the rubbish will be removed from Bellingshausen Station with the help of our Russian friends and corporate sponsors. The waste will be recycled or disposed of in accordance with best environmental practice. *2041* will begin a major city world tour with education as the key message. Ten young teachers from around the world will visit Antarctica and plan an educational out-reach programme.
SPONSORSHIP & SUPPORT RAISED TO DATE = £5.87 million

PAST EXPEDITIONS

1986 'In the Footsteps of Scott'

From a young age, Robert Swan was inspired by the Antarctic and in particular Robert Falcon Scott's voyages to this last great wilderness on Earth. After studying History at Durham University, Robert started to plan his own expedition 'In the Footsteps of Scott' and seven years later, after six years of planning and one year spent in a hut on Antarctica, he successfully reached the South Pole on foot.

Cost of project £3.5 million
Main sponsor: Shell UK
Secondary sponsors: Burberrys UK, Barclays Bank plus 1,500 additional sponsors

1989 Icewalk

There was now one thing left to do - to reach the North Pole. Robert Swan, together with seven fellow explorers from seven different nations finally arrived at the North Pole in March 1989, after a long struggle across melting ice. This achievement made him the first person to have reached both Poles on foot. The expedition further involved 22 young people from 15 nations working together at Eureka, the Canadian environmental weather station, directly participating in the scientific research and learning about the fragile Arctic environment.

Cost of project £4.7 million
Main sponsor: Amway Japan
Secondary sponsor: Yomiuri Shinbun Japan plus 450 additional sponsors

1996/97 Tandem One Step Beyond

Back to the South Pole, Robert Swan continued where he left 10 years ago, attempting the first ever complete crossing of Antarctica. Together with two fellow explorers, he went One Step Beyond, using equipment never successfully used in the Antarctic before. Robert then joined 35 young explorers from 25 nations on the expedition ship from South America back to the Antarctic, leaving his two team members to finish the crossing and thus allowing himself to keep his promise to the young explorers.

Cost of project £1.7 million
Main sponsor: Tandem Computers Inc USA
Secondary sponsors: Bata Ventlex UK, Robert Swan Foundation UK, Reuters UK, plus 250 additional sponsors

ROBERT SWAN, OBE, BA, FRGS

AWARDS

1987	Citation of Merit from Explorers Club of America
1987	Fellow of the Royal Geographical Society
1988	Polar Medal - awarded by H.M. Queen Elizabeth II
1989	United Nations Global 500 Award
1989	Appointed United Nations Goodwill Ambassador with Special Responsibility for Youth
1990	Citation of Merit from Alpine Club of Japan
1991	Paul Harris Fellow of Rotary International
1992	Peary Medal from Ski Club of Great Britain
1992	Visiting Professor for the School of Environment, Leeds Metropolitan University
1993	Doctorate of Letters, The Robert Gordon University
1995	OBE - awarded by H.M. Queen Elizabeth II
1995	Vice President of the Countryside Management Association
1997	Council Member, WWF (UK)
1998	Smithsonian Award for Information Technology in Education & Academia
2000	President of the Captain Scott Society

If you have the desire for knowledge and the power to give it physical expression, go out and explore. If you are a brave man you will do nothing, if you are fearful you may do much....

Apsley Cherry-Garrard
"The Worst Journey in the World"

MISSION ANTARCTICA
Yacht & Expeditions

Crown Street Chambers, 2/4 Crown Street,
Darlington, Co. Durham, DL1 1RN, UK.

Tel. 0044 (0) 1325 462041
Fax. 0044 (0) 1325 462601
E-mail. MA@2041.co.uk
Web site: **missionantarctica.com**

Contacts ~ Adrian Evans, Managing Director
Angus Buchanan, Logistics
Bronco Lane, Expeditions
Garry Evans, Technical Manager
Hugh Bernard, Voyage Co-ordinator
Lennie Watson, Personal Assistant
Emma Buttle, Merchandising Co-ordinator

2nd NATURE LTD.
Robert Swan speaking engagements

Crown Street Chambers, 2/4 Crown Street,
Darlington, Co. Durham, DL1 1RN, UK.

E-mail: alex@2041.co.uk
Web site: **www.2ndNature.co.uk**

Contact ~ Alexandra Imholz